UNDERSTANDING THEISM
101

UNDERSTANDING THEISM
101

A Starting Place For Making Sense Of Christian Faith And The World

DARRIN CROW

XULON PRESS

Xulon Press
2301 Lucien Way #415
Maitland, FL 32751
407.339.4217
www.xulonpress.com

Paperback ISBN-13: 978-1-66285-627-3
Ebook ISBN-13: 978-1-66285-628-0

Contents

Acknowledgments

I want to offer my sincere thanks to the following people:

My wife Stephanie, whom I do not deserve.

My son Liesen, who shares my mind and love of wit.

My daughter Blythe, who shares my heart for the broken of this world and the need for good advice.

My parents, Gordon and Betty Crow, who raised me with a mind for ethics.

My friend and coworker Zach King, who does things at church so I can write.

My friend Jordan Haren, for providing the cover art and chapter illustrations.

My friends Vicki Tucker, Elizabeth Bush, and Ashley Reed, for advising me regarding the content of this book.

Emma, Jordan and Tori, Travis, and Mattie, who bring games and laughter to our home.

My church, HEART of Junction, for simply being an awesome encouragement to me through the past quarter of a century.

All of the students I have enjoyed knowing over the years at Christian Challenge at Colorado Mesa University.

The students who took my classes at Colorado Christian University, I hope you remember some of this stuff!

The Facebook people (it says they are my friends!) who responded over the years to these posts, encouraging me to keep at it.

My two most significant spiritual mentors, Chip Collins and Max Barnett, who tried to bring wisdom into my life. Thanks for trying!

Introduction

Years ago I was asked to teach a class called Worldviews for Colorado Christian University. I was thrilled to do this because Worldviews was one of my favorite undergraduate classes.

I was also preaching at the church we had planted; and even though I was only supposed to pastor our church until we got a real preacher, it has now been twenty-four years of talking to a roomful of mostly interested people every week. Then along came Facebook, my only foray into social media. Most of my initial Facebook contacts were folks from the church and my classes at CCU. These, then, were my three worldview audiences: college students, church members, and Facebook friends. My nature was to take on a pastoral role with all three crowds, seeking to teach and encourage.

One day I posted a thought to Facebook that I titled "Understanding Theism 101." I do not remember exactly what my first post was about, but I know I was trying to explain why Christians do some of the things that Christians do, right or wrong. To my surprise, I got a lot of feedback and conversation from that post. For a while, we kept that conversation going. People asked questions and made comments, and I responded with more thoughts, explanations, and declarations. That first conversation quickly escalated to include more than two hundred exchanges!

A key response was posted by a friend who was not a theist. She was blown away that a discussion about a divisive core belief could have such a lengthy dialogue without a single angry response. She thanked me for being pithy and charming while expressing serious opinions. She remarked that I could be self-deprecating not only about my own character, but about the general faults and failures of my tribe. She felt like that transparency allowed her to reciprocate.

That interaction with my friend encouraged me enough to put up a second post, and then they just kept coming. For a while, I was still focused on responses and conversations around the posts, and I usually kept the discussions going for at least several days. I liked the conversations and encouraged them, almost always with pleasant social results. It was obvious there was a group of people who were interested in learning more about worldviews, especially from a Christian perspective.

Eventually I started posting mini essays regularly and worried less and less about the length or depth of the conversations the posts generated. My goal was always to present truth and be open to the fact that Christians may be hard to understand because of the things they believe and because of the way they often fail to live up to their own standards.

I eventually added new posts only occasionally, usually prompted by politics or some dumb preacher somewhere. Facebook started to get a bit mean for me, and I retreated to simply reposting some of the original posts when they came up in my online memories. Over the years, it was suggested to me by people I trusted that I should put these together and do something with the posts. I let cancer and other stuff take that thought away until earlier this year.

So here it is. I found about three hundred different posts out of who knows how many. I kept about 120 of those posts and then organized them as well as random essays may be organized. Then I filled in some blanks. My goal was to help you to know more about what you already know, to help you live your truth in grace toward yourself and others, and for you to have a fun time on the way.

I hope what results is worth your time.

Blessings,
Darrin

Chapter 1

Thoughts on Worldviews

I have traveled overseas thirty-four times. With more than twenty trips to the former Russian state of Belarus, and more than ten trips to Kenya, I am familiar with the cultures and people of these two countries. They could not be more different from each other. Most of my American friends simply do not relate to the stories I share of Nairobi slums or Belarusian villages. To attend church in either place would be an unusual experience for even the most churched among us. Yet if you are a Christian, you are likely to see the world very much like Belarusian and Kenyan Christians. You would think more like them than you would many of your neighbors in America. This is because of worldviews.

You are likely familiar with the old story of the blind men trying to describe what they experienced as they each touched a different part of an elephant (Saxe). Each of six different blind men described an elephant based on the small bit they encountered. None of them were able to describe the whole elephant because they were each limited to the data allowed by their limited experience. The man who experienced the tusk had a much different understanding of what an elephant is as compared to the one who felt the ear, and so on. The moral of the poem is that we tend to develop an absolute truth from a limited perspective. This is a good picture of how most of us approach our first encounter with worldviews. We are blind to many insights that our friends might have, and they are blind to what we know. We are limited by our perceptions, and we may erroneously determine absolute truths based on incomplete data. Learning about worldviews is a way to make sure we are seeing the world as clearly as we are able and at the same time learning a bit about why our friends have different understandings of the world than we might have. As much as possible, this book will serve as a first attempt to see the whole elephant.

The content of this book beyond the current chapter is mostly part of a series of regular posts on my Facebook wall over the past decade. There were a lot of folks who offered interesting feedback to many of these postings that I have not included in this compilation. There are often references to events that were current at the time of the post but are history to the readers of this book. The posts were not written in any particular order and are admittedly written to differing levels of academic rigor, all the way from "see Jane run," to complex discussions of vague academic terms. These mini essays are generally simplistic in nature. Each essay could lend itself to thousands of words, whereas I usually use hundreds of words. Even though they are minimal explorations about a variety of thoughts, they should not be dismissed lightly. Though they are highly generalized, each thought is a summary of a larger topic. Taken in whole, they develop a comprehensive though far from exhaustive volume on the broader topic of theism in general and biblical theism in particular.

These readings will help to provide you with a cursory understanding of the theistic worldview. This is *Understanding Theism 101*, which is a much different thing from graduate studies on the topic. Before we get to the mini essays, let us begin with some clear thinking on theism and worldviews in general.

How Do We Define Worldviews?

In academics, the discipline of worldviews is taught through many different worldview lenses. There is no real consistent lexicon from which to draw. I will use terms that are familiar to many scholars of worldviews, but other scholars might use other terms. My defining norms are consistent with those I used as part of the curriculum when I taught classes on worldviews for Colorado Christian University. The primary texts that were used at CCU were James Sire's *The Universe Next Door* (2009) and a wonderful book called *Making Sense of Your World: A Biblical Worldview* (Phillips, Brown and Stonestreet 2008). I strongly prefer the latter's definition of terms.

All of that said, please understand that it would be easy and likely fair-minded for a person to take umbrage at my groupings, categorizations, and titles of worldviews. This would be especially true if that person fit into one of two camps: those who know a lot about the topic and those who know very little!

It would be fair to ask why it is even necessary for you to distinguish worldviews at all. There are several important reasons. The first is that you no longer live in an isolated world. You work with and relate to people from a vast array of understandings. You need not agree with everyone, but respect should be enough of a reason to try to understand somebody else before simply dismissing them. A second reason for understanding theism, if you are a Christian, who I suspect will amount to 99.9 percent of my readers, is that you need to strive for coherent integrity in your life. Socrates would tell you that the unexamined life is not worth living. He may have been a little extreme, but I can guarantee that the examined life will create less hell on earth for anyone. Blessed is the person who takes advantage of the opportunities provided by insight.

WORLDVIEWS

A HUMANIST	A SKEPTIC	A THEIST
A DEIST	LGBTQ+	A GNOSTIC
AN ATHIEST	A PANTHEIST	A BUDDHIST
A POSTMODERNIST	A NATURALIST	A FAT WHITE GUY FROM GRAND JUNCTION

SEE THE WORLD FROM SOMEONE ELSE'S POINT OF VIEW

Are Theism, Deism, and Monotheism All the Same?

They are almost the same thing. Theism and monotheism are the *exact* same thing, meaning that the basic presupposition is there is one personal God who created everything from nothing. Deism fits within the worldview of theism because in deism the presupposition is that a single God has become disinterested after kicking things off and has subsequently left the game. Deists deny the idea of special revelation by Scripture or an encounter with God. A few of my posts mention deism, but every post that mentions theism is also talking about monotheism. It is simply an abbreviated version of the word.

Other theistic worldviews, such as pantheism, polytheism, and panentheism, *are not* the same as theism. God is redefined in these expressions in such a way as to make them distinct from theism. This is an important distinction to keep in mind as one considers worldviews.

Does Everybody Have Biases?

We cannot begin to discuss worldviews intelligently until we recognize that each one of us have biases built in to our awareness of the world. There are many kinds of biases. One simple example is that recent events and trends are easier to remember and discern than either events in the distant past or unknown events that will occur in the future. This is known as recency bias. It stands in contrast to historical bias or memory bias. These biases show up when sports fans try to determine the G.O.A.T. (greatest of all time). It is hard to compare Babe Ruth to a twenty-one-year-old phenom of the week, but when folks argue online about these things, they are often unaware of their bias. We have all sorts of preconceived ideologies that we use to decipher the realities of the world. Different cultural and incidental forces have combined to form a person's understanding of the world and its inhabitants.

Everyone is biased, especially preachers and scientists. My particular biases include male American, politically conservative, socially liberal, heterosexual, *theistic* Christian Baptist (Southern), non-Reformed, late baby boomer/early buster Caucasian with an affinity for Irish rock music. That is just for starters! What are yours? Some of you might recognize your biases by how you respond to my biases. If you are politically progressive, you might be naturally repelled by some words I use in describing my biases. But this is how people overcome disagreement in order to communicate. It is only by seeking first to understand, and then by seeking to be understood, that we can ever actually learn and move in our intellect.

I confess my bias to frame my claims and the perspective from which I write. Even though I will touch on other worldviews and on several religions that are not my own, I am really hoping to be understood as a biblical theist and to help you understand biblical theists (aka Christians).

If you are Christian, Muslim, or Jewish, these little synopses *should* describe and hopefully explain your behavior and thoughts to a small degree. If your personal worldview is something other than theism, these ditties might help you to understand some of your friends a little better. To those readers who are Christian, remember that simply calling yourself a Christian does not mean that your thoughts and actions are Christian, or even theistic. What I am trying to describe in the following pages is authentic theistic behavior and understanding. Authentic biblical theistic behavior is defined by our sacred text and historical understandings. Feelings, current trends, and culture do not inform theistic thought. I truly hope that you are challenged by some of my observations. I often use terms such as *practicing theist* to distinguish true theism from some of the errors we believe, live, and present to the world. My thoughts are mostly true and mostly helpful toward living a life of integrity. You do not have to agree with my conclusions, of course, but I hope your arguments against these thoughts are based on true things.

I really want to encourage my nontheistic friends to catch hold of a big idea that I was forced to address very often when these posts were being discussed online. When I share how a practicing theist should see truths, ideas, societies, and cultures, I am simply trying to express that all of the inbuilt biases a theist would have are going to produce these viewpoints or view of the world. I believe them to be true, but they will likely not be the same conclusions somebody with another worldview would reach. So rather than screaming at the page that Darrin is wrong or bigoted (I might be, but it is not worth the effort), simply realize that this might explain a bit of why your theistic family and friends think the way they do. It has always been difficult for we Christians to defend our observations to nontheists because we look at things from different perspectives. Worldview conversations are conversations about the disagreeable. Let us take some of the heat out of the conversation by admitting this from the beginning.

Are Worldviews and Religions the Same Thing?

Theism is a worldview, not a religion. Several major world religions, including Islam, Judaism, and Christianity, share a theistic worldview. Sikhism, Eckankar, and the Bahá'í faith are theistic as well, but I will address these religions only briefly. Though these religions would likely agree with many of the theistic generalizations being offered in this work, they each have significant distinctions that make them less relevant to the conversation.

One way to understand this concept is to consider that the same worldview of extreme Islam that allowed for the 9/11 horrors also allowed for the Christian Crusades and the crucifixion of Christ at the hands of the Jewish chief priests and rulers. We all feel like God is righteously angry about some behavior or another, and so our extreme group members seek to make corrections no matter the cost. It is much rarer to see these extreme behaviors in other worldviews.

If you begin to look at worldviews through the magic eye of internet searches, you will find that some of the people who are the most interested in the subject are Christians. Many of them will speak of a super-tight framework for the "right" worldview, and it is distinct from any other religions. They are usually defending a Christian worldview, or a worldview that they might call Christian theism. Many of them do not want their Christian rice to touch the Muslim corn or the Jewish peas. I think this one plate of food constitutes a single worldview, and though the differences are huge, they are distinctions lying within an enormous common ground. The right class to make those distinctions would be Religions 101. You could dig even further into the Christian rice portion of that plate and spend plenty of time in another class called Christian Denominations 101. I am writing about worldviews. It is silly to be offended by the fact that we share common ground with Judaism and Islam. It is helpful to know the common ground as well as the distinctions.

We All Have a Worldview, But What Does That Mean?

Everyone has a worldview, but very few realize that is the name for their perception of the world in which they live. Even fewer know or understand the implications of their worldview. People simply do not think about it. Fox News and CNN present the world through different lenses. Fox watchers think CNN is arrogant, and CNN viewers think Fox is ignorant. Both sides always think they really told the other side off in every debate. These mega news outlets are worldview holders speaking to worldview adherents.

You have a worldview, as does your neighbor, your president, your teacher, and the pastor at your church. Comedians and artists have worldviews. Every one of your children's teachers has a worldview. The people who make your favorite movies and television shows have worldviews. The editors of your local paper and favorite magazines have worldviews. Your doctor and your therapist have worldviews. Your wife and children have worldviews, and they might not share your worldview.

This is all very important. You would think that since facts are facts, we could communicate quite nicely when we lay out all the facts on the table. But that does not happen because even though a fact seems static and unbending, the worldview lens through which we view that fact can cause two people to reach different conclusions about those so-called facts, just like the blind men and the elephant.

An example might be, "It is a fact that we should raise our children lovingly." Anyone who disagrees with that would be suspect, and we might not want to let them coach a kids' soccer team. However, because of worldview distinctions, one parent's loving interpretation of this fact might be applied by not expecting the child to participate in household chores because they do not want the children to feel any sense of oppression. Another loving parent might lovingly interpret this fact as it is applied to the question of chores by concluding that children need to learn to do hard things even when they do not want to do hard things, because it is a part of self-mastery. This is more than different parenting styles. It is brought forth from how these parents answer worldview questions.

How Do We Discover Our Worldview?

Our worldview is defined by the way we answer basic questions about the nature and operating principles of the world in which we live. We do not get to choose our worldview, and some people will be offended by this. Our worldview describes what we actually believe. Our behavior betrays our belief, and our belief betrays, or defines, our worldview.

Even if you have never discussed or directly thought about these basic worldview-defining questions, were you to be faced with these questions, you would probably already know your basic answers. These known answers to unknown questions are called presuppositions.

These questions include the following:

1) Is reality knowable or unknowable?

2) Do you believe in a god, or gods?

3) Do you believe in the supernatural?

4) Where do you think stuff came from?

5) What do you believe about the nature of time?

6) What is a human being?

7) What happens to us when we die?

8) How do we know right from wrong?

9) What is evil?

10) How do we know anything at all?

11) What is the meaning and purpose of life?

12) Is history directed or undirected?

These questions are hierarchical in nature. This means that the first questions will tend to divide a population into subgroups, and the following questions further divide the subgroups into smaller groups. It does not work to scatter the questions or to use them in reverse order unless you are simply using the questions to challenge yourself according to your assumed worldview. As you work your way through some of these worldview questions, your individual set of presuppositions will sift you through a series of pigeonholes to a personal worldview. Most people find themselves solidly in one of about eight or ten different possibilities. A few folks will be all over the board, answering some questions theistically and others atheistically for instance. These folks might find themselves struggling to function well in key areas of life. That is just the way it is when your worldview lacks internal consistency.

This book is primarily concerned with theism. Christians, Jewish people, and Muslims will answer these questions nearly identically. Let us look at our questions again, this time with typically basic theistic answers:

1) Is reality knowable or unknowable? *Knowable.*

2) Do you believe in a god or gods? *One God with personality.*

3) Do you believe in the supernatural? *Definitely. God is beyond nature.*

4) Where do you think stuff came from? *God made it.*

5) What do you believe about the nature of time? *There was a beginning of time and will be an end. Eternity exists outside of time.*

6) What is a human being? *A purposeful creation of God that somehow contains elements of God's personality. Life began only once, thousands of years ago when God breathed life into man, and life is passed on, life unto life.*

7) What happens to us when we die? *We continue to exist. We face a judgment: heaven or hell.*

8) How do we know right from wrong? *Partially from observing natural law, mostly from revealed law (Bible, Qur'an, or Torah). Our moral compass is external, not internal.*

9) What is evil? *Ruined good. Evil is a consequence of not following God's plan for us.*

10) How do we know anything at all? *Created nature and time provide an environment for us to connect with God.*

11) What is the meaning and purpose of life? *To connect with and to be made right by God; to recognize our created purpose.*

12) Is history directed or undirected? *It is directed by a sovereign God. It is linear, but without beginning or end. Time is contained within, like eternity is the paper on which the finite timeline is drawn. History is meant to reveal the solution to our individual and corporate search for God.*

Now let's compare the simple theistic responses to these questions to those of another worldview. Let us answer from the perspective of a naturalistic atheist:

1) Is reality knowable or unknowable? *Knowable.*

2) Do you believe in a god or gods? *None.*

3) Do you believe in the supernatural? *No. Nature is all we have.*

4) Where do you think stuff came from? *From the big bang. Matter must have always existed in some form or another.*

5) What do you believe about the nature of time? *It has always existed.*

6) What is a human being? *An accidental, evolutionary development. Individual human beings have no special inherent value beyond the fact that they have conscious awareness.*

7) What happens to us when we die? *Oblivion.*

8) How do we know right from wrong? *Observation and evolved social conditioning and constructs.*

9) What is evil? *Bad fortune that could happen at the same statistical rate to anyone.*

10) How do we know anything at all? *Scientific method, reason.*

11) What is the meaning and purpose of life? *Ultimately, there is no meaning, but individual meaning might be extrapolated.*

12) Is history directed or undirected? *Undirected. The evolutionary law of survival of the fittest rules. It is linear, without beginning and end.*

In both sets of responses, our answers are simplistic but adequate to see accurate distinctions. We can understand that other worldviews, such as nihilism, humanistic atheism, pantheism, spiritual existentialism, and polytheism, will each have a particular grouping of basic answers to these questions. I have included some of these in the appendix for a further comparison of worldviews.

Worldview discussions *are not* theology discussions. Even biblical theism cannot be boiled down to a term as simple as *Christianity*. Many religions fit into the category of biblical theism, including Catholicism, Protestant Christianity, and many other forms of extrabiblical theism, such as Jehovah's Witnesses and Mormonism. There is also a growing subcategory that may be called edited biblical theism, in which the adherent chooses to consider less than the entire biblical record. It should be remembered that as you read each *Understanding Theism 101* post, a tiny fragment of theism is being revealed. In many cases, these revelations are broad and could be speaking of Christianity, Judaism, or Islam. In other cases, I will make distinctions between the three religions that are borne out of similarities. A Christian and a Muslim might say "this is how we differ," while a humanistic atheist would think that we are discussing only a distinction but not a difference.

How Do We Evaluate Worldviews?

Worldviews must always be evaluated. There are many good ways to check for validity in the way you see the world. These tests would include the following, at a minimum:

Is my worldview able to offer an explanation of everything without major gaps? It takes a lot of work to confirm that a worldview can contain a comprehensive explanation of the world, man, nature, and thought. In her blog, Carmen LeBerge (How to test a worldview, 2022) asks us to consider four big ideas: (1) origin, or where do we come from? (2) meaning, or why are we here? (3) morality, or what is right and what is wrong? and (4) destiny, or where are we going?

One of my goals with this book is to present theism in general, and biblical theism in particular, in order to provide a framework that offers a comprehensive answer to our questions regarding the nature of the universe, our minds, good and evil, and time and eternity, everything that we encompassed in our preconceived answers.

Is my worldview free from internal contradictions? Is it free from logical inconsistencies? I must test my worldview by determining that there is a sense of integrity within my understanding of how things are. Therefore, many of the posts will contain a reference to authentic theists, or authentic biblical theists. The authentic biblical theist will challenge inconsistencies such as claiming that all people are intrinsically good, when the Bible clearly states otherwise, when empirical evidence clearly states otherwise, and when our own hearts and minds clearly know that we ourselves are not even good.

Does my worldview contradict reality? Some people would argue that biblical theism at its very core contradicts reality by introducing God into the argument. A reason for this book is to present bite-sized samples of how straw-man arguments against theism are challenged by a more mature argument, such as the distinction between the natural world and the supernatural world. Biblical theism embraces paradox and offers understanding to these big questions.

Can my worldview be lived out? Is it doable? Life is difficult enough without throwing unattainable expectations into the mix. Again, a reason for this book is to help us make sense out of true biblical theism in the face of less than authentic expectations of God and Scripture. For instance, if our worldview of biblical theism were to wrongly include the idea that God answers every prayer with a resounding *yes,* well, that is simply not going to jive with reality. My worldview has to connect with my actual experience.

What is the Connection Between Worldviews and My Soul?

The biblical theist believes that there is a part of us beyond the intellect and mind which is capable of knowing. It is different than feelings and different than what we mean when we talk about our heart. This part of us is called the soul. The soul can be wounded and broken, or it can be strengthened and encouraged. The biblical theist believes that truth and scripture nourish the Christian soul. Untruth and scriptural ignorance weaken the soul. Meditation upon the precepts of scripture provide understanding, insight, and emotional freedom. It is the soul which experiences peace, and it is the soul that is crushed by chaos. The intentional work of striving for intellectual integrity sets the soul's house in order. These thoughts tidy up our existence.

How to Read This Book

These writings are organized into chapters that correspond with the basic presupposition questions from this chapter. There are many posts that could fit into various chapters, as they touch on multiple issues. I have done my best to group them according to the biggest ideas. They are meant to be stand-alone thoughts that might be worthy of meditation or reflection. Some posts are grouped together because they were posted as a series. The first several posts offered in chapter 2 are presented together because they provide a bit of a framework for worldviews in general. Chapters 3 through 14 correspond to the presupposition questions, and chapter 15 is a collection of posts that concern practical applications.

Since this book is a collection of short essays, it might be more beneficial to some readers to read the essays in small bits of just a few at a time. Please remember that when I wrote most of these essays, I was presenting them at the rate of one essay every few days. I figured that one thought with some conversation was plenty to chew on at one time! Now I am presenting an entire basket of thoughts. Although I would hate to describe this book as a "bathroom reader," the truth of the matter is that this might be the best definition of the book. The key idea is to remain connected to the chapter headings, and only read until you stop absorbing.

There is extraordinarily little Scripture mentioned in the posts, and the distinction between theism in general and biblical theism is randomly interspersed. There are occasional references to other worldviews, especially as comparisons, but this book is written to explain and understand theism, especially biblical theism, in bite-sized chunks. Some of the posts are entirely dedicated to Christian thought. Other posts are more generalized. There is an appendix at the end that briefly discusses other major worldviews.

Please remember that theism is a broad worldview that covers multiple religions. Some common ideas or thoughts might show up in multiple places. Usually there is enough of a twist to have made it worthwhile to keep some nearly identical essays. The good news is I discarded about two-thirds of the posts! So those that remain follow...

Chapter 2

Introducing Theism and Worldviews to Your Thinking

These posts are generalized thoughts about theism and do not fit into the categories that speak more precisely to the presuppositions from chapter 1. In this chapter, I will define some terms and introduce several comparative positions from other worldviews. I will take several opportunities to distinguish worldviews as separate from but connected to religion. Ready. Set. Go!

Understanding Theism 101: I have a friend. We have been discussing the fact that my posts tend to overgeneralize, and perhaps unfairly. Let me say a word or two about worldviews. Worldviews are about beliefs, not about people. Worldviews pigeonhole us by dragging us through a series of questions that we are predisposed to have opinions about, even if we have never seriously thought about any of the questions. We just seem to know the answers to questions like, Do I believe in something beyond nature? A *yes* puts me on one side of the fence, and a *no* puts me on the other side of the fence.

The questions continue:

> Do I believe in God?
> Has matter always existed?
> What is the nature of time?

How do we know right from wrong?
What happens when we die?

CHOOSE YOUR FATE

There may be multiple answers to these questions, but humanity will divide into somewhere between seven and thirty major groups that could be identified as worldviews. The best thing about this is applying the realization that I see things from a different perspective than does my neighbor. It is obvious that I can communicate better with people if I understand myself and if I understand them. There is no value to one worldview above another until we use our understanding to communicate more fairly. This allows us to pursue truth together. What a neat thing!

Theism is the only worldview that has a sense of urgency to recruit from the other worldviews because theists think that we continue to exist after death, and we are going to have to answer to God. A nihilist would only recruit toward their worldview for intellectual stimulation or company.

One last overgeneralized thought about worldviews: They are not religions. Theism, for instance, includes the three major competing religions: Judaism, Christianity, and Islam, and several less-major religions. I hope this helps. All I am saying here is this: sometimes nontheists do not even try to understand a theist's point of view, and sometimes theists do not even try to understand the point of view of other worldviews. I think we can all have good reasons for how we answer those basic questions.

Understanding Theism 101: I just had an interesting conversation with a friend who left theism in recent years and ventured into a different worldview, most probably agnosticism (people who believe we cannot know what we need to know in order to know for sure) or perhaps atheism. The difficulty of moving from one worldview to another carries with it a lot of relationship baggage. I think the crux of the question is this: why is it so hard for theists to let the rest of the world believe what they want to believe?

I would first say that practicing theists, the ones who are doing theism and not just preaching, are worried for everyone else. They believe the bridge is out and souls are in eternal, immortal danger. I appreciate agnostics, like Penn Jillette, who are understanding of the love that is behind this sort of hollering that we do so well.

I would also say that practicing theists should be okay with allowing others to have different beliefs, religions, or worldviews, even though we are afraid for their destinies. I say this because in all three major theistic expressions (Islam, Judaism, and Christianity), God is understood to allow these things. In all three expressions, the bad news is that God literally burns the universe of anything anti-theistic in the end. This sounds terrible, but it is the essence of theistic cosmic justice: choose the right side. For those who say this is completely vindictive, please temper this with the idea that God is allowing us to choose. It seems to me that a great respect is shown to the created by the Creator in this freedom to choose against Him. I guess, and I wonder, which would be worse: to choose against God or not to be allowed to choose anything? If God gives me the choice to reject Him, who am I to refuse that choice to somebody else?

I care, and I hope that when I reach for you with desperation and clumsiness, you might at least know it is because I want you to be safe. But if you do not believe, you do not believe.

Understanding Theism 101: Monotheism means pertaining to a belief that all creation flows from one God who has a mind and intentionality. Monotheism and theism are the same *Understanding Theism 101* conversation. In these posts, I often use the term *practicing theist*. This term refers to a person who thinks, behaves, and responds from a theistic point of view. A person who believes they are a theist simply because they go to church, or they like the idea of Jesus, or they like spiritual things may not in fact be a practicing theist.

This is about more than simply being a hypocrite. There have always been people who attach themselves to a religion for show without ever intending to live up to the expectations of the religion. This is done for political or social reasons, or perhaps to secure relationship status or money. Hypocrites are simply hypocrites, and they are not a surprise to anyone. The behavior of a hypocrite does not prove or disprove anything.

I am speaking more to the people who generally desire to function in the religious tradition with which they identify yet find themselves frustrated with intellectual and emotional connections to that religion. They recognize inconsistencies between their claimed worldview and how they see things. Part of my desire with these small essays is to challenge us to rethink some of these inconsistencies and perhaps find that we can be intellectually honest with ourselves.

Understanding Theism 101: Theism cannot be defined by the behavior of hypocrites who claim to be religious but fail to follow the basic tenets of theism. Theism defines us—we do not define theism. Theism is a set of coherent answers to a complex series of questions about the nature of existence. Grouchy preachers and rich prophets may claim to be devout biblical theists, but they may be operating from another worldview position and are lying in order to fleece some fatted lambs. You must not dismiss out of hand the theistic worldview simply because of the poor behavior of those who claim the idea for themselves. You can dismiss the hypocrite as either a liar or a fool, but not the worldview. You must use the terms of the worldview in order to dismiss the worldview.

Understanding Theism 101: In many of my posts on theism, I am quick to mention there are many points on which all types of theists generally agree. This is true, and to non-monotheists, these generalities overshadow the distinctions between the religions that share a monotheistic worldview.

Some distinctions, however, pit theists sharply against one another. One of these differences between the religions centers on what it takes to be right with God. In the Jewish faith, there is no belief that people must be naturally evil, bad, or sinful. The process of getting and being right with Yahweh is essentially to keep the Law, or to follow prescribed procedures to keep from making Him angry, and then to be purified in case of a failure.

For Christians, it is impossible on their own effort to be right with God because He is perfectly holy, and any mistake we make demands a permanent separation from God. That is harsh, but God knew about this problem and provided a cheat-code in the person of Jesus Christ. Embracing His sacrificial death, burial, and resurrection and submitting oneself to making the will of God our highest priority can put us in right position with God.

In Islam, there is a similar sense of submitting to rules and seeking to live according to the will of Allah. A sort of scorecard is kept, and if at the end of life you are in the positive, you will be saved. Sins and obedient acts are weighted, so a white lie may not be too damaging, but a lie that sends a family into poverty or a person to the grave may be impossible to overcome.

Why would theists put up with an almighty deity that makes things so hard? Well, we wouldn't if we didn't believe in Him. But we do. Not liking God is not a good enough reason to not believe in God. So that's it.

Understanding Theism 101: I often refer to the three big religions of monotheism: Islam, Christianity, and Judaism. There are several other semi-major religions that fit less comfortably into the theistic worldview. Let us present a sentence or two about some of these other religions just so we know a little bit more than we did before.

The Bahá'í faith is a relatively new but growing religion. The primary teachings involve an appreciation for the best things that other world religions have to offer. Bahá'í prioritizes human unity. It developed in Iran and the Middle East in the last two hundred years or so. These guys are easy to befriend.

Another fairly new religious sect is Sikhism. Founded in the 1400's and common to India and Pakistan, Sikhism is the fifth-largest religion in the world according to Wikipedia. God is revealed through the teachings and meditations of respected gurus. Meditation, sacrificial service, and the prosperity of all humankind are foundational. My favorite hospital in the Nairobi slums is a Sikh hospital. They have helped us to minister to the poor on multiple occasions. They have also cared for injured and sick American missionaries.

Eckankar is super new, even newer than me. An American twist on Sikhism, Eckankar adherents connect with God via meditation and seek to free the soul from the body. Yeah, I don't know one either, but they are big in Minnesota.

Zoroastrianism is much older than these Johnny-come-latelies. Pushing three thousand years of history, this religion is monotheistic, but it is difficult to summarize core beliefs or a central theology. An eternal struggle between good and evil fought by angels and demons with a general wish for equality and the best for humankind seems to be the best I can do in a few sentences.

Another twist on theism is that the broad category can include religions that we would describe as extrabiblical. Mormonism would fit into this category. Mormons are monotheistic and likely relate to a significant portion of these posts but have several additional texts that are held as revealers of God's will and direction. Jehovah's Witnesses are not strict biblical theists because they hold that many orthodox understandings from the biblical record are significantly flawed. So close, yet different.

Understanding Theism 101: The three major world religions by number of adherents all fall under the broad canopy of theism. Some of my friends are offended by this idea, thinking there is no greater difference in the world of thought than the difference between Christians and Muslims. Others are offended by the possibility that Jewish people, Christians, and Muslims worship the same God.

It is true. These religions are vastly different, and our understanding of God separates us from faith-fellowship entirely. We should still be able to have lunch with anybody, but it is very unusual for our three faiths to intermingle. We disagree on lots of details. To a naturalistic atheist, however, we all appear to simply be three kids in the same family fighting over whom Dad likes the best.

Understanding Theism 101: Regarding biblical theism, you will see me refer to either practicing theists or authentic biblical theists. A question that has been asked several times is, "Darrin, are you saying that an authentic biblical theist *is* a Christian?" There are many people who claim to be Christians who do not desire to practice biblical theism reliably or consistently. We have a word for such people—hypocrites. Others do not practice all things well, but authentically seek to practice well. We have a word for these people—failures. Others practice theism very well but have never surrendered lordship to Christ. We have a name for these people—legalists. Others practice the faith authentically and with surrendered hearts. We have a word for these people—followers (of Christ). Is it possible for a hypocrite or a failure or a legalist to be a Christian? Are all followers Christians? Are all Christian practitioners saved? Wow, lots of questions! Let me say two things that are meant to help sort this out. First, biblical theists *must* concede that the only way to be saved is to allow Christ to do the work of saving us. We can't save ourselves. Second, we can never know the mind and heart of another person.

I leave this post with a couple of obligations. The first is to remove from my own life any obstacles to obtaining and living truth. That is the very best way to feel secure in my faith. The second obligation is to help remove those same obstacles in the lives of others with grace and truth. The goal is always to alleviate suffering rather than to judge.

Understanding Theism 101: I am writing about theism as opposed to religion or theology. A lot of topics for future posts have been suggested, but most of them are particular to theology and tend to distinguish the world religions from one another. The world religions are different, but I have not been writing about differences. I am writing about sameness.

One question posed to me should be addressed: what is the point of the *Understanding Theism 101* posts?

My point for these posts is threefold: (1) I want theists to think about their biases and presuppositions, (2) I want nontheists to consider a little bit of our perspective, and (3) I want to begin to answer the best question of the 1990s, Rodney King's "People, I just want to say, you know, can we all get along?" (USA Today 2007). The answer to Mr. King's important query is, probably not. But with fairness and a little insight as to the other person's point of view, *some of us* can get along better than we currently do. I hope you have been getting something positive from the posts regardless of your personal worldview.

Understanding Theism 101: A worldview is a lens setting through which we see the world. There are crazy people in every worldview population. Crazy is as crazy does, and crazy people act out according to their worldviews. Crazy in the theistic worldview is always damaging to the reputation of God. When the boogerheads from Westboro Baptist Church gleefully attach God's name to tragedy, this is not a theistic expression. It is simply crazy. When two Chechen immigrants blow up 180 people at a marathon in Boston to express a point, it is not theism. It is simply crazy.

If you are not a theist, please do not evaluate theism by the crazies who attach themselves to it. I will show you the same courtesy by not evaluating atheism according to the personality flaws of Richard Dawkins, or nihilism according to the politics of Adolph Hitler.

Understanding Theism 101: One of the best explanations of worldview is that it "is a commitment, a fundamental orientation of the heart, that can be expressed in a story, or in a set of presuppositions (assumptions which may be true, partially true or entirely false) which we hold (consciously or subconsciously, consistently or inconsistently) about the basic constitution of reality, and that provides the foundation on which we live and move and have our being" (Sire 2009, 20).

As I have been sharing Theism 101 insights, I have often used the phrase *practicing theist*. I have done this to distinguish between those whose general belief and behavior are theistic and those who simply think they are theistic because they like the meta narrative that spins from the God story. I guess we could say about theism and all worldviews that we do not define theism—it explains us.

Many of my students in the worldviews classes that I taught at Colorado Christian University were surprised to find out that they were theists. They were unchurched and often angry at God, yet they began to realize that their presuppositions were specifically theistic. Others discovered that despite their churchy backgrounds, their presuppositions defined another worldview, most usually secular humanism, a non-God, spiritually tinted worldview.

Understanding Theism 101: The second question that I ask people to consider is this: do you believe there is a god or gods, or do you believe there are no gods? This question has a correct answer, but only one correct answer. The other answer is wrong, and what we believe about it does not change the answer. I am just making a logical statement about the question. I am not arguing it one way or the other right here.

For most of us, we have never thought deeply about why we suppose that we know the answer to this question. Most of us arrive at the answer early in life, and then we build support for our supposition throughout the years. It is not uncommon for the events of life and observations and conversations to move us from our original position on this question. But it is important that we consider this question rigorously. Blaise Pascal, a big-time thinker, offered his opinion on this question by positing what is now known as Pascal's wager (Pensées 2002 (uploaded pdf), 35-45). He said that even though we could not know with absolute certainty that God exists, human beings wager with their lives whether God exists or not. His own conclusion was that we should seek to live as though He exists, just in case He does, and further that we should attempt to believe in Him just in case He exists. It was Pascal's form of probability theory being used to mitigate risk. Theists love to play Pascal's card in discussions regarding God. It might not be fair, but it makes sense to my theistic mind.

Agnostics are put in a tough spot when it comes to the first question. They can openly admit there is indeed a correct answer regarding the god or no god(s) question. The problem is that they believe there is no way to know the answer. I know agnostics who live as if there is a God and others who live as if there is no God. I think they are at their happiest when they are not thinking about it!

Understanding Theism 101: Every now and again some of the questions that arise from these posts must deal with other religions or worldviews. I was asked recently how theism relates to Buddhism and Hinduism. These two major world religions, along with Taoism, Scientology, and Wicca, all fall under the broader worldview of transcendentalism.

The basic presuppositions of transcendentalism descend from a ladder of awareness that includes the ideas that ultimate reality is knowable and spiritual, and that we can transcend the world as it is to create the world as we want it to be. Ideas such as illusion and karma are huge in this worldview. There is a strong spiritual connection that may be shared with the thinking of theists, but a distinct difference is that theists are bound to the realities of a single god's direction. This is why Unitarians are not theists. We are not kicking them out; it is just what it is. It takes more than a church building to identify a worldview.

A further distinction for theists to understand is that every time I use the word *theism*, it is one and the same as the more precise *monotheism*. This means we believe in one God who is personal in nature. Transcendentalists may be polytheistic (many gods), pantheistic (God is everything), or even animistic, which simply means that objects, places, and creatures have a spiritual essence or life. New Age adherents fit into the transcendental camp as well.

Understanding Theism 101: Any worldview should be able to offer a big T.O.E (theory of everything). It has been suggested that an adequate T.O.E. will include at least four major components (LeBerge, 2-3). I will look at these four big ideas in this post and the next several posts.

All worldviews should address the idea of origin, or where did we and where did stuff come from? This question has puzzled philosophers since Thag Simmons stared into the night sky while devouring a brontosaurus burger and pondered the great question about the chicken and the egg. There are bonus points for anyone who knows who the late Thag Simmons was (Patoway 2020).

The universe is puzzling, from its dimensions and vastness to the basic question of where it came from. If something exists, it had to begin to exist, right? Naturalistic atheism suggests a big bang. I just read an essay that suggested seven possible naturalistic explanations for the origin of matter. Every single theory began with the assumption there was some sort of matter or thing that had to be present at the beginning (Kumar 2020). Most spiritual worldviews suggest a supernatural influence that caused things to begin.

All forms of theism have within their sacred writings noticeably clear expressions of the way things began, along with the two most important answers to the two big questions. First, who or what was the first cause, and then, what did the first cause set into motion? In biblical theism, our big book of what God says begins at the beginning in the aptly titled section called Genesis. God, who always existed, spoke matter into existence from nothing. From that matter, He created the earth and the universe and the natural laws that define it. Furthermore, He took that matter and created man.

This seems like a major cop-out to anybody who subscribes to any of the naturalistic worldviews such as humanism or naturalistic atheism. But one of the biggest questions that divides worldview adherents is the question of the supernatural. Theists believe there is a realm beyond nature. We have an obligation to prove that assertion, but that is for another day. Right now, just know that your friends who are theistic are pretty sure it is no sillier to believe in the supernatural than it is to believe that the best explanations of where stuff came from is to begin with the assumption that there was already some stuff.

Bonus: A bunch of scientists decided that they could now create life in a laboratory and that God was no longer needed. So they sent a team of representatives to God to present their findings and to ask God to please butt out once and for all. God said that would be fine if they could create life out of a handful of dirt like He did once upon a time. The scientists conferred and decided they could do that. The challenge was on, so they scooped up a handful of dirt and smugly set out to take on their task.

God said, "What are you doing?"

"Well," they said, "we are going to create life out of this handful of dirt."

God said, "Get your own dirt."

Understanding Theism 101: Continuing with the idea of origin, the first question that begins to shape worldview identity is, Where did everything come from? Theists think God made stuff. This seems oversimplistic to other-than-theistic worldview adherents, especially atheists. But atheists have a problem here—a big problem. Let me quote *Washington Post* scientific editor Joel Achenbach: "So, then, why is there something rather than nothing? There just is. The is-ness of the universe is one of its interesting features. Sorry if that isn't satisfactory. It is because it is. Let's move on" (2013). Pretty scientific, huh?

Theists catch a break here, as our response, theoretical for sure, at least deals with the breakdown of the problem: cause and effect. Since nothing happens that is not caused to happen, we think something happened that was not caused to happen, just like Achenbach thinks. But he limits his conclusion to what he can learn from the natural world. We expand to the supernatural—God.

God, rather than the universe, is the uncaused first cause of everything. Before Hubble and his telescope, science was okay with "everything was always here." Now, with Einstein's theory of relativity and expanding universes and such, atheists need a big-bang, something-from-nothing approach to postulate. This is fine, but Achenbach himself states that the reason his "just is" approach is legal is because theists use the same approach to proving God (Ibid.). Fun, huh?

Understanding Theism 101: In recent posts, I discussed the need for our worldview to address a comprehensive theory of everything (the big T.O.E.). We spoke about origins, and now I want to consider the question of meaning, or why we are here (LeBerge). We also discussed the idea of stuff. Again, to weakly summarize the view of the most diametrically opposed worldview from theism, atheistic naturalism suggests that ultimately there is no meaning—we are one of a billion cosmic accidents, and when the universe collapses, it will all be for nothing. Humanistic atheism tells us that amid this cosmic accident, there is great meaning if we can squeeze it out from a life that begins in the cradle and ends in the grave. Things like books and movies, poetry and art, and family legacy can pass meaning from generation to generation. Robin Williams summed this worldview up nicely in his worm-food speech from *Dead Poets Society* (Weir 1989).

Theists in all three major expressions generally find that meaning for our existence is to be derived from some personal communication from or connection with the mind of God. He has a plan for man in general, and me, specifically. We find the general plan for all of us in His revealed Scriptures, and His specific plan for me through meditation, prayer, and circumstances. This is why so much of the stuff that theistic extremists do seems completely crazy to the rest of the world, things like following God's plan to clean up the world from sin and error by blowing something or someone up. Hmmm... that *is* crazy.

Biblical theists will often answer the question of meaning as it relates to the purpose of Jesus Christ and His revelation of Himself in our awareness. For instance, He claims we find meaning by believing in Him, trusting in Him, submitting to Him, and most surprisingly, suffering with Him. That last one is such a big thing. Those of you who are not theistic in your worldview have likely questioned your theistic friends' willingness to suffer and even die for what they believe. Jesus tempers the crazy thinking by asking us to die *for* others rather than making them die for us.

Understanding Theism 101: My last few posts have been taking on the challenge to address the theory of everything (big T.O.E.) We looked at origin and meaning, and in this post, I want to briefly discuss the idea of morality (LeBerge). Every worldview should have a tight understanding of what is right and what is wrong. Boy, do we theists have this one pegged! We have commandments, laws, and rules out the wazoo.

Worldviews that do not contain a God narrative use this question as a sledgehammer when taking on the integrity of the theistic worldview. It is easy to see there is a lot of wrong in the world, and especially easy to see that bad things happen to innocent people, whether natural bad such as an earthquake or cancer, or unnatural bad such as a dictator or drive-by shooting. It has been argued that theists declare that God is all-powerful, all-good, and all-loving, but since evil exists and people suffer, then God is not all-powerful and can't defeat evil, or He is not all-good and does not care about evil, or He is not all-loving and does not care about our suffering. Therefore, God does not exist (Russell 1957).

Biblical theists have a lot to say about this. It may be briefly summed up this way: everything that is broken in the world will be made right in time. God is not fixing everything right now because He is giving us time to choose to trust Him, because as C. S. Lewis has said, "Once the author walks onto the stage, the play is over. The time for choosing has gone" (Mere Christianity 1952, renewed 1980, 28).

Sacred texts inform theists about right and wrong. That is why theists do not bend well to pressure to accept nonsacred current moral absolutes. An authentic biblical theist distinguishes between what is nice and what is helpful when thinking about love. There is not any room in biblical theism to think that Jesus never judges people regarding sin. He said it Himself, that at the end of the age, He will separate all people into two groups: one bound for hell, the other bound for heaven (author's interpretation of Matthew 25:31-46). How He decides is a conversation for another essay, but He will decide. His own summary is love God and love others, but I think He defines love in an action sort of way. At my church, the sign says, "Love is meeting needs." I usually say it is more loving but less nice to tell someone they have spinach in their teeth than it is to not say anything. In fact, in theism niceness is not even a virtue. Kindness is a virtue.

One last thought: The naturalistic worldviews do not get a pass on the nature of evil. In the most basic of naturalistic expressions of what evil is, the conclusion must be there is no such thing as evil, only good and bad things that happen at statistical rates to everyone. But even my most scientific friends think that a murderous pedophile is truly evil. William Lane Craig and Peter Atkins have debated this question wonderfully (Cumming 2008). You should watch that conversation.

Understanding Theism 101: Let's conclude this miniseries on the necessity for a worldview to adequately answer the need to contain a comprehensive theory of everything, or big T.O.E. We have looked at origin, meaning, and morality and have now come to destiny, or the question of where I am going (LeBerge). Worldviews must address the issue of what happens at the end of our lives.

Biblical theism speaks to this question from our sacred texts, which we believe to be the revealed word of God. It begins with essentially bad news. The story is that we have become disconnected from a holy and perfect creator, and that our destiny is not only to experience hell on earth because of that, but to experience a permanent separation from God after we die, even while we continue to exist in an eternal supernatural reality (C. S. Lewis, Mere Christianity 1952, renewed 1980, 78). But the reason Christians call the central message of Jesus the "good news" is because we may be saved from this disconnection with God. The first verse that anybody learns from the Bible is John 3:16: "For God so loved the world that he gave his one and only Son, that whoever believes in him shall not perish but have eternal life" (Scofield 1984, NIV).

The other two major theistic religions are similar in consideration of the question of our destiny. Other worldviews include ideas of destiny as ultimately ending in a manner that would be called obliteration. It is funny how many of my friends who do not believe in the supernatural use phrases like "He passed on," or "Mom is watching over me." I have always liked this quote: "'Never tell a child,' said George Macdonald, 'you have a soul. Teach him, you are a soul; you have a body.' As we learn to think of things always in this order, that the body is but the temporary clothing of the soul, our views of death and the unbefittingness of customary mourning will approximate to those of friends of earlier generations" (Peckham 2012).

Understanding Theism 101: If you are an atheist who is trying to make sense of theism, or at least trying to make sense of your theistic friends, recognize that your own operating system is not compatible with theism. Theists and atheists are like Apple and Android: we can talk to each other, but we can't share the same operating systems. We have different presuppositions. Theists believe in the supernatural, while atheists do not. Theists believe in directed history, while atheists believe things are undirected. Theists believe in life after death, while atheists do not. These presuppositions go on and on and are way beyond the basic god or no-god question. Just as there are multiple religions that share the theistic operating system, there are multiple strains of atheistic thought as well.

The naturalistic atheist is concerned about the practical answers of scientific inquiry and usually has no real reason to fight with another person regarding worldview. Think of Carl Sagan or Stephen Hawking, who has recently entered the debate with a silly effort (The Grand Design 2010). Just being a world-famous theoretical cosmologist does not make everything you say true.

The humanistic atheist sometimes looks like a theist or at least a spiritual person because of their love not only for humanity, but especially for the individual. Think of almost any character Robin Williams ever played. *Dead Poets Society* (Weir 1989) is the humanistic atheist's version of Mel Gibson's theistic *The Passion of the Christ* (2004).

The anti-theist is a strange worldview offshoot. Anti-theism, as opposed to a-theism, is a worldview that is literally defined by what a person is against. What makes it interesting is that what they are against is something they do not even believe in. The basic mistake anti-theists seem to make is that they evaluate theism entirely from the framework of atheism. There are some neat anti-theistic websites. I like 500questions (500 Questions about God and Christianity 2012) and whywontgodhealamputees (Brain 2012). The questions that are asked on those sites are good, but they do not destroy theism for a theist. They only explain why atheists are not theists. Theists have different presuppositions.

Understanding Theism 101: Fifty years ago (originally posted on 11/22/2013), two of the twentieth century's greatest writers passed away. The deaths of Aldous Huxley and C. S. Lewis were barely noted, however, because this was also the fiftieth anniversary of the death of John F. Kennedy. If you want to take a challenge, you have 365 days to read *A Brave New World*, *Mere Christianity*, and *Profiles in Courage*. This fiftieth-anniversary intellectual pleasure cruise is brought to you courtesy of the day the grim reaper drew an ace-high royal flush on a three-card draw.

Peter Kreeft (Between Heaven and Hell 1982) has authored a wonderful little book about this odd coincidence and explores Lewis's theism, Huxley's pantheism, and JFK's existential humanism.

Understanding Theism 101: This post is for my theistic friends. I want you to understand something about your friends who claim to be agnostic. We often think of agnostics as head-in-the-sand, unwilling-to-take-a-stand types. Sometimes we feel that agnostics simply will not apply themselves to the question. Agnostics *are not* people who do not know whether or not there is a God. Agnostics believe that we *cannot* know whether or not there is a God. This is a huge difference emphasized by all the italicized words. Agnosticism is intellectually honest. As such, agnosticism is not really a worldview of its own; rather, most agnostics default into either humanistic atheism or naturalistic atheism at the worldview level. You do not need to prove to an agnostic that God exists; you need to prove to him/her that you *can* prove that God exists. That is tough, but possible. My best approach is to talk about things that are immeasurable but solid, things like justice, love, beauty, or fairness. Those are our closest connections to the supernatural that other worldviews might recognize at least on a metaphysical level. I think some agnostics would say that these types of abstract conceptual realities dissuade them from tagging themselves with the atheism label. I hope this rings true to my agnostic friends.

Understanding Theism 101: Practicing theists tend to be very divided by religious lines. In fact, there seems to be a further distance between Jewish/Christian, Jewish/Muslim, and Muslim/Christian than there is between a theist of any brand and any other worldview adherent. In my expression of theism, biblical theism, we divide even further until we have reached the point of literally thousands of documented denominations and sects. We each must be very careful in our pursuit of religious truth not to think we have found it perfectly.

"Sis-boom-bah! Go, Southern Baptists! We're number one! We have spirit, sure we do! We have spirit, how 'bout you?"

Understanding Theism 101: Two expressions of theism that are quite contrary to biblical theism, as well as the theism of Judaism and Islam, are the worldviews of deism and finitism. Deism, in a nutshell, is the belief that God exists but basically has little or nothing to do with the world and those in it. He started things off and checked out. A small minority of our Founding Fathers were deists, and their deism was an offshoot of theism. Steven Hawking (Hawking, A Brief History of Time, 10th Edition 1998) and Albert Einstein (Viereck 1929, 60) make lots of noise that sounds deistic when talking about the beginning of the universe. For the record, they normally defaulted to agnosticism when pressed, and Hawking was married to a biblical theist who demonstrated love he could not fathom.

Finitism is the belief that God exists but his powers are limited, especially in the face of the question of evil. It sounds like the groundwork for a big Superman-versus-God battle for Lois Lane's immortal soul. The only value to most of us regarding today's post is that pure theism should not be confused with deism or finitism.

Understanding Theism 101: The internet is full of conversations between theists and naturalistic atheists. Most of these conversations are rancorous at best. In almost all cases, it is easy to observe the breakdown in common ground. The theist does not understand that the atheist does not believe in "super" natural, and the atheist does not understand that the theist does believe that there is a nature beyond. It is like watching people argue in two languages. I have spent enough time overseas to see this happen a lot.

> Theist: If something exists, it had to begin to exist.
> Atheist: So, what?
> Theist: The universe had to begin. God did it.
> Atheist: Does God exist? Who made Him?
> Theist: I'm going to kill you and your momma!

Atheist: That's what she said...

Okay, many of the internet arguments are better than this, but only slightly. As a theist, I think it is funny when an atheist uses the "no supernatural" gig on this conversation, then later moves to alternative universe proposals with different (aka, supernatural) natural laws than those we know in our universe. I am sure we make the atheist laugh a lot as well, perhaps when we say God is love and then verbally napalm anyone who says differently.

Respect is cool.

Understanding Theism 101: Blaise Pascal (Krailsheimer 1966, 32) once wrote, "The heart has reasons that reason cannot understand." Every worldview should be able to withstand a rigorous evaluation process, and one important test is the test of the heart. This means that your personal worldview needs to stand up to subjectivity. Theists have this one kicked. We are famous for subjectivity and usually claim it to be objective. This test of inner reason (Phillips, Brown and Stonestreet 2008, 56) could never stand alone, but it is necessary as a portion of an overall evaluation. Basically, the question is, Is my worldview satisfying at a gut level? Many theists are not emotionally satisfied with theism and over time drift away from religion. This is common in all worldviews. Our parents raise us one way, our heart rebels, and we move toward a worldview we can practice wholeheartedly.

I would argue, of course, that we drift away from things other than theism while thinking it is theism we are rejecting. This is the old baby-and-the-bathwater problem, and many former theists eventually long for the baby again. A few examples of reasons people leave biblical Christianity are as follows:

"I can't believe in a God who lets people suffer."

"All the church wants is money."

"I prayed sincerely for grandmother to be cured of cancer and God didn't deliver."

None of these things are true from a biblically theistic perspective, but we've made cartoons out of how we think about things. There might be answers to these tough questions if we were to look deeper.

Understanding Theism 101: The worldview that stands in direct opposition to the theistic worldview is atheism. There are several variations on the atheistic theme.

Naturalistic atheists are what I like to call straight atheists. Their foundational viewpoint is formed around natural laws and observable experience, and they rely exclusively on the scientific method. They are not inclined to enter debates with theists unless it is for fun or simple academic pursuit. They are not naturalists because they eat wood or love the environment more than they love their mothers; they simply have no room in their real experience for the supernatural, a mandatory concession for any type of theistic worldview.

Agnostics are sometimes made to appear to be silly because they do not know what they believe. While it may be true that some agnostics are simply vacant of deep thought, more often the case is that these folks are undecided based on evidence. Agnostics serve as a valuable reminder to those of us who are so firm in our worldview propositions that we refuse to see other perspectives. There are a lot of smart people in this world who are not sure. In fact, most people who call themselves agnostic are thinking deeply about these questions. I categorize them with the atheistic worldviews because of the "little bit pregnant" factor. You can't be a little bit theistic. I think that is funny.

Humanistic atheists (sometimes called *existentialists*) basically hold to most of the same principles as naturalists, but they differ on the nature of human beings, believing that the human experience is the ultimate concern of existence. Humanists often have a spiritual but nontheistic bent on things. Love, for instance, may be transcendent. Many Robin Williams movies where he tries to be serious (*Patch Adams* (Shadyac 1998), *What Dreams May Come* (Ward 1998), *Dead Poets Society* (Weir 1989), etc.,) probably fit this worldview. Many nonpracticing theists float here when they move away from their faith.

Anti-theists is a term I made up to describe those folks who are simply dishonest or angry theists, or just mean people. Guys like Richard Dawkins or the local nut job who screams about the Ten Commandments and Nativity scenes fit this description. Scientific method is abandoned to manipulation. Truth-seeking is void, and position-proving is paramount. Theists have their counter to the anti-theist. Usually we call them preacher, rabbi, or imam. Not all religious leaders fit this description, but many, many do. Honesty and love go a long way in the pursuit of truth.

Understanding Theism 101: Theists love dealing with questions of origin, such as, Is there a God? By definition, theists think the answer to this question is yes, but many worldviews answer this question in the affirmative. For instance, pantheism, panentheism, new age, deism, and polytheism all assert there is a god. Theists believe some specific things about the nature of God that are distinct from other worldview approaches, such as God is personal, eternal, creative, and active. The characteristic that is the most important to consider regarding the theistic view of God is that He exists outside of nature. He supersedes nature... supersedes nature...supernature...supernatural...ta-da! By the way, pick a side and get involved in the three-hundred-year war about whether it is spelled *supersede* or *supercede*.

Theists believe God is beyond nature. Thus, if you think as does the famous *luchador* Esqueleto, who said, "I don't believe in God, I believe in Science" (Hess 2006), the theistic view of God is eliminated from the beginning. But if you believe in some unmeasurable possibilities beyond the natural, such as love, beauty, or justice, you may connect with the theistic heart.

Understanding Theism 101: The last few days I have posted about the idea of origin and the question, Is there a God? Theists think there is a God. I googled the question, Why do people think there is a God? The first listing, by *Way of the Mind*, listed eighteen reasons he claimed were typical answers for why theists believe there is a God. The only ones I could relate to were number two (personal experience) and number eighteen (God is an explanation for unexplained things) (Kren 2006). Most of this list includes things such as assumptions that Christians are ignorant, uneducated, and indoctrinated.

I will be the first to admit that many theists have few good reasons for believing in God. That does not mean there are no good reasons for believing. I mentioned the "uncaused cause," which was a favorite of Thomas Aquinas. C. S. Lewis proves the existence of God through a conversation on fairness (Mere Christianity 1952, renewed 1980, 11). N. T. Wright does the same thing by discussing our concept of justice (Simply Christian: Why Christianity Makes Sense 2006, 41). Leading atheist Frank Morison was converted to Christianity when he attempted to disprove God through a legal analysis of the New Testament writings (Who Moved the Stone? 1930). Josh McDowell uses internal consistencies of the Old Testament and messianic prophecy to validate his conclusions (The New Evidence That Demands a Verdict: Fully Updated to Answer the Questions Challenging Christians Today 1999). Lee Strobel was converted from atheism when he used his degrees in law and journalism to conduct investigative interviews with scientific experts (The Case for a Creator 2004). William Lane Craig uses Aristotle's logic to defend the existence of God (Biola 2009). Charles Colson went from convicted Watergate conspirator to a long life of ministry to prisoners around the world as he weighed suicide against the claims of Christ (Born Again 1976). There are a lot of smart people who believe. I wish *Way of the Mind* were interested in really tackling some serious arguments, but sadly this website may have perished with the times.

Understanding Theism 101: Practicing theists are rarely aware that they are operating from within the context of a worldview. This is true of most of us, regardless of our worldview. The one person who is most singularly defined by their worldview is the atheist. The rest of us prefer to understand ourselves in the context of religion, politics, nationality, or culture. Atheists are just lucky that way in the sense that in worldviews discussions, they are not defined by what they believe, but rather, they are defined by one particular thing in which they do not believe. It would be like defining me as an a-unicornist.

Theists usually are very unaware that their basic presuppositions about some of life's most important questions are shared by adherents of three of the world's greatest religions. The big ideas of theism generally agree with the sacred writings of these three religions: the Torah, the Qur'an, and the Bible.

Understanding Theism 101: Oh, man. Today I was looking at a chart that FEVA Ministries (2011) has online. They have adapted worldview categories from James Sire (2009). There is an added worldview called *apatheism.* It is a worldview defined by apathy concerning the God question as related to meaning and life.

At first, I thought this was a worldview for stupid people. The chart identifies the first decade of the twenty-first century as the beginning point for this new worldview. The people it describes seem to believe that if there is a God, He does not care about fairness, goodness, or us, so the heck with Him. It seems to me that this is a temporary landing spot for people who have been disillusioned by the big theistic religions. I guess time will tell.

Understanding Theism 101: Yesterday I mentioned the questionable worldview of apatheism. What a great debate that post inspired! There was lots of testimony about how people lost their faith. Several folks were far from apathetic about their theism. Let us see if today's post hits the nerve again or if I can explain a concept that was brought up in the emotional debate that was presented yesterday.

When teaching worldviews at Colorado Christian University, I always take a bit of time to make the distinction between atheism and anti-theism. After yesterday I will add apatheism. Anyway, atheism is simply an unemotional worldview that is completely disconnected from the idea of a supernatural deity or deities that created and interact with the world. Anti-theism is a worldview founded upon an anger against a God who has been rejected or an anger with a rejected religion. An atheist does not think much about God unless he sits too close to a theist at a party. An anti-theist is always ready to tell the world why God does not exist. I do not think anti-theism is a worldview as much as it is an attitude.

Chapter 3

Theism and the Nature of Reality

The first question we asked in helping us to determine our worldview was this: is reality knowable or unknowable? Theists believe, along with many other worldviews, that reality is knowable. We believe that what is real may be observed and understood. We believe this stands in distinct opposition to the idea that we cannot know anything for certain.

Understanding Theism 101: Theists believe that reality is knowable. We share common ground on this question with all our favorite nontheistic worldview expressions, such as naturalism (atheism, humanism, hedonism, etc.), transcendentalism (pantheism, polytheism, animism, Unitarianism, etc.), and even our own theistic black sheep of a disappeared cousin, deism. Until the last twenty years, the push against an unknowable reality was limited to some far-out readers of Derrida and Foucault. A few prophets foretold the impending move from modernism to a place called postmodernism. That's silly, we all said.

Well, postmodernism is here, and it is here in a big way. Truth is no longer absolute.

"Well-l-l-l-l," he said in a southern drawl, "that depends on what the word *it* means...."

We now live in a world where postmodernism has won the cultural battles. Older people who do not watch news or social media may not even know there are more than two genders now. Reality is challenging when we cannot figure out how many restrooms public buildings need to provide in order to keep everyone safe, and that the new women's NCAA swimming champ needs a better bikini to hide what modernists still call a "bulge."

Postmodernism is here for a while, though some still believe it will eventually crash in around itself into a giant pile of word casserole. There is a great advantage to believing that truth is ultimately not knowable. Adherents to the belief get to claim that every other worldview and every practice of the worldview is nonsense. The crumbling moral high ground upon which that belief allows them to stand must eventually give way to the fact (knowable!) that postmodernists must use argument (knowable!) to defend their positions (and, knowable!).

It is a worldview, but not a tenable one. Don't embrace it for the kindness it supposedly offers.

Understanding Theism 101: When considering worldviews, one of the first dividing lines comes in how we answer this question: is ultimate reality knowable or unknowable (Phillips, Brown and Stonestreet 2008, 16)? Almost all people will answer this question in the affirmative, and it is the most common ground that theists share with their atheist friends. Enjoy that common ground, because we can sit side by side and wonder in amazement at what all those postmodern types are thinking. The major worldview positions for those who believe reality is unknowable are pragmatism, antirealism, perspectivism, and antiessentialism. We are looking mostly at literary positions such as deconstruction and speaking about guys like Dada, Foucault, and Derrida. You should google Derrida.

One further thought about those who can make theists and atheists agree on something. This group of people can be identified by their secret club password: mytruthisdifferentfromyourtruth.

Understanding Theism 101: What does it mean that reality is knowable? It seems obvious at first. Is that not why we call it reality?

In years past, this was a no-brainer, and I mean that precisely. Our brains (or minds) were not part of the equation, and for thousands of years, this made things easy, especially when combined with the fact that a very high percentage of the world was illiterate. But the printing press and university system brought forth an age of enlightenment that sent the philosophers into orbit. One Prussian soldier couldn't help but wonder, while he was supposed to be on guard duty, how he really knew anything existed at all, including himself. He finally concluded, "I think, therefore I am." And with that, Rene Descartes changed the world.

Before that, most of humanity thought that their god or gods were the great I AM. Theists have a God who even called Himself the great I AM. Jesus died because He kept repeating that He was the great I AM. When Descartes said *he* was "I am," everything moved from "God is who *He* says He is" to "God is who *I* say He is." With this we were ushered into the modern world. Five hundred years later postmodernism moved us to "God is nothing more than an idea."

Understanding Theism 101: Practicing theists believe that God is infinite. He is not bounded in any way by space or time. Sire calls the nature of God the "really real" (2009, 38). This idea that God is the most real part of our reality is joined in some degree by the pantheists and polytheists. It is the opposite of some worldviews, such as naturalistic atheism, which holds that the main reality is cosmic matter; the stuff the universe is made of is all there is and all there will ever be. Nihilists agree there is nothing beyond the material that makes up the universe. Humanistic ultimate reality is a negative - God does not exist. The worldview that might be the most fun when it comes to prime reality would be the postmodernists. They claim that language functions are the way that meanings are constructed. At the same time, they also live to deconstruct meanings, so there really is no such thing as "really is."

"There really is no 'really is'" would make for a great T-shirt.

Understanding Theism 101: Reality may be defined as that which is knowable. The problem with reality is that sometimes we think we know something to be true, *but in reality,* we do not know that thing. Consider a man who believes he has a strong marriage, but he is deceived to the fact that his wife has three unknown lovers and a deep desire to kill him for the insurance money. Boy, that got dark.

Theists understand that we live in a world in which we may be easily deceived. Biblical theists believe that we have a spiritual enemy whose nature it is to look for opportunities to deceive us. Kathy Bates called him the "debil" in *The Waterboy* (Coraci 1998).

So what provides us with our best grasp on reality? Biblical theists choose to let the mind of God be their most secure resting point when determining reality. Do I feel like an idiotic loser? God says I am the light of the world. Do I feel like I am not accepted by others? God says I am His child. Do I feel like I am condemned by God because of my failures? God says there is no condemnation for those who are in Christ Jesus. The truth is more than idealized wishes about God. Theists believe that reality is revealed in scripture rather than feelings.

Understanding Theism 101: When theists think of what is real, they face the same crisis as everybody else, the slippery slope of feelings. For practicing biblical theists, the most ardent will treat feelings as something akin to the check-engine light on the dashboard of a car. That light is a warning for us to recognize that something is wrong and we better see what the *real*(ity) problem is. It is not enough to simply be sad or angry because of what may be happening. It is time to focus on what is really happening and make solid decisions about how to proceed in such a way as to alleviate future pain and discomfort.

The reason that practicing theists believe in pursuing facts over possibly untrue or unhelpful feelings is because they believe in an absolute truth. Biblical theists even have a verse that tells us that if we abide in the truth, we will know the truth and the truth will set us free (John 8:31, 32).

This is not to say that feelings are bad. After all, feelings warn us of problems. Even with happy feelings, though, check out what is really going on. Falling in love and feeling horny are both going to excite happiness, but they are remarkably different in guiding us toward wise decision-making.

Understanding Theism 101: The ultimate reality for theists of all three major religious groups is that *God is*. For theists, everything about reality is understood from this starting point. The biblical text begins with, "In the beginning, God..." We agree with many other worldviews that reality is knowable, but we immediately take a turn away from much of the rest of humanity by putting God in the mix.

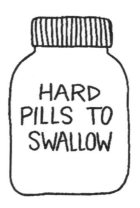

Understanding Theism 101: One of my friends who is not a theist has commiserated with me on one of the greatest difficulties about the questions we deal with in these posts. Is the word *God* capitalized or not? I have tried to be consistent, but it sure does not appear that way. For the record, I capitalize on the occasions when I am speaking of the God of theism, and I use lowercase in occurrences that are speaking of polytheistic gods or pantheistic gods. This is not meant to be a put-down; it is just a respect for the personality of the theistic God as opposed to the nonpersonal gods we also mention.

Now, for the capitalized personal pronoun debate. I think He wants me to capitalize "he" when I'm speaking of Him.

Understanding Theism 101: Often our friends who hold other worldviews dispute our desire to base our understanding of reality upon a God who does not exist within the nature of reality. Theists believe that God exists both inside *and* outside of nature. We believe that God created all the natural world, and that He still lords over all of creation. We believe that if God desires, He can cause the winds to blow or the rains to fall, even when the weather forecaster says differently.

Biblical theists take this a step further by rejoicing in the story of the supernatural God humbling Himself to become one among the created. He lived and died as a man and defeated the reality of death by rising from the dead after three days. It is not only one of our best stories, but it is the centerpiece of our faith.

Understanding Theism 101: There is a distinction that should be made regarding reality. Reality is the basis for a major separation between pantheists such as Hindus, and theists. This distinction says there is the reality of what God is and the separate reality of what God is not. Pantheists believe that God is everything. Theists believe that God is distinct from that which He created. Theists believe that God is omnipresent, or everywhere, but do not believe that He is the substance of that which He created.

Understanding Theism 101: If, as theists believe, we are created in the image of God, that is a reality that must effectively overwhelm our entire understanding of what is real. The touch and signature of the Creator is upon every child born into this world. If that is the case, the theist is by necessity obligated to care for and nurture the creative touch upon everyone, fanning it into flame.

Wait. Dang. Who am I supposed to hate? A practicing theist is obligated to love everybody. Everybody is a lot of people. The most anger I ever generated on Facebook came when I made the outrageous claim to my Christian friends that no matter who your neighbor voted for in the Trump/Biden election, Jesus is asking us to love them anyway. It seemed obvious to me, but I found out that a lot of people who claim to be biblical theists do not care what Jesus said.

Understanding Theism 101: Several of my posts regarding the nature of reality have expressed the idea that for the theist, God is the ultimate reality. It is worth distinguishing that God is not only a reality, but He is also a divine reality. This means that for the theist, God is the rule maker and definer of terms. If He says something is right, it is right. This makes it a bit difficult for those of us who want to set ourselves up as the proclaimers of right and wrong. Theists defer to their sacred texts. Timothy Keller once said that if we think and behave exactly as our God does, our God is nothing but a glorified version of ourselves (Sermons 2019). I think that is an amazing thing to think about.

Understanding Theism 101: *Do not* try to understand theism from the perspective of the History Channel. The reality of God is reduced to ancient alien astronauts, and nothing else.

Understanding Theism 101: Theists understand reality in such a way that the emerging practice of cancel culture cannot be embraced. Cancel culture, for those of you who are fortunate enough not to know, is also known as call-out culture. Cancel culture, or call-out culture, is a current phrase used to refer to a form of ostracism in which people are removed from social or professional circles, whether it be online, on social media, at a job, or in person. Those subject to this ostracism are said to have been cancelled. The ostracism results from any behavior or vocalization of disapproved positions.

There is a sense in which theists can appreciate the big idea behind cancel culture, that marginalized people might finally have a voice. It seems like biblical theists might recognize that Jesus is for the marginalized. The problem is, Jesus is also for those who come from a position of privilege. Pay attention—I did not say He was *for* privilege.

One of the two favorite places humans in general like to position themselves is within the category of innocence. We tend to think we do not need to use the air freshener after a number two. The other favorite landing spot for most of us is to see ourselves as victimized. Victimization is such a dear, comforting friend, but theists believe it is a wolf dressed in sheep's clothing. Victimization tells us that our issue, ailment, or tragedy is not our fault. This is often true, though not always. If it is not our fault, our status as a victim gives us permission to fail or to be angry or rude. Some victims of oppression, real or imagined, love to scream at their oppressors. Victimization may become a person's primary identity, and this may destroy beautiful truths that are veiled by the victim identity. Victimization allows for the comfort of fellowship with other victims within tribal identities.

If we think we are blameless, or if we think we are excused by our victim status, we find ourselves willing to make declarations about the vacant morality or virtue of the guilty or the oppressive. These are often highly punitive declarations, such as "fire them," "send them to jail," or "injure or kill them." At least burn down their businesses or their neighbor's business, or, "what the heck—let's burn it ALL!"

Biblical theists are oriented around loving neighbors and enemies. That pretty much cancels cancel culture if we are going to take our biblical theism seriously.

Understanding Theism 101: I remember being impressed by the story that concerned the grand opening of Disney World, the grand upgrade of the highly successful Disney Land. It was remarked that it was too bad Walt Disney had passed away before the park was opened. He would have loved to have seen it. Walt's wife, I'm told, said, "He did see it. That is why it is here."

That just makes a lot of sense to me when we think about theism in the context of reality. We believe we are in process of becoming the "really real." Part of my reality is that I am not yet what God desires me to be, not during my time on this earth and especially not after I transition from what I am now to what I will ultimately be after I die.

This is called vision. I do not think that vision is unique to theism. In fact, it should be something that almost every worldview other than nihilism should embrace. The theistic spin is worth reflection. For the theist, the vision of what his/her reality can ultimately be is painted by God. Theists always know they are getting themselves into hot water when they decide what is best for themselves.

Chapter 4

Theism and Belief in God

The second question that we ask in determining our worldview is this: do you believe in a god or gods? Theists believe there is one God, and that God has a mind, a conscience, and a personality. He does intentional things on purpose. The image of God as a giant, white-robed old man floating in the heavens is the result of Renaissance art. We generally have decided that God's preferred pronouns are He and Him, but that is mostly literary convention. Both male and female are created in His image, and the Psalms talk about His wings, so we must be careful when putting too much or not enough into our understanding of His nature.

Understanding Theism 101: Each of the major theistic expressions does a different thing with the person of Jesus Christ.

Islamic theists believe that Jesus was a prophet, even a great prophet. His words are respected and revered. He was not the greatest prophet, nor is He God. He is highly respected, and His teachings are to be obeyed.

Judaic theists believe that Jesus was a false prophet. The tension in the Gospels between Jesus and the Jewish leaders was what eventually got Him into that whole cross episode.

There are many people who do not fit neatly into any one worldview. They like Jesus Christ as a moral teacher or as a great example but reject him as God. This is odd. He claimed to be God. That is why he was killed. C. S. Lewis (Mere Christianity 1952, renewed 1980, 29) said He was either a nut job, or He was a liar, or He was who He said He was—God; but to say He was just a great person is "patronizing nonsense."

There is another group of folks who do not fit into any one worldview who appreciate Jesus and the God part but reject the Old Testament God. This is silly as well. Jesus said that He and the Father were one, and He was speaking of that Old Testament dude. Those who take the "Godness" of Christ but reject the Father fail to maintain the standards needed for worldview integrity, because they are denying a basic claim of the sacred text.

Biblical theists believe that Christ is God. He was the fulfillment of Old Testament prophecy. They believe He was a prophet, powerful in word and deed before God and man. They believe He rose from the grave alive—He was not a zombie. Most importantly, they believe that when Jesus talks about love, the most important detail is that His love is backed with the power of God—resurrection power.

Understanding Theism 101: Practicing theists believe that no matter what is going on in the world, God has not lost control. The worldview that supports the failed or absent God theory is called deism, and those folks basically feel like God started things off, left a few good ideas, but became disinterested. Nihilists, such as Nietzsche and Hitler, generally feel that God was an idea whose time came to an end through the enlightened awareness of a few special people.

The implication of theistic belief is that if God is in control, and if it appears that at the same time chaos reigns, then God has allowed this chaos but will eventually put things right. This partially explains the political and social-moral fervor of theists, especially biblical theists. We have decided that God either needs or simply wants our help in noticing things and putting them right. When a theist takes a stand on abortion, poverty, or immigration, it may be either out of love for the injured and innocent or simply out of a desire to do right things. "Stop abortion!" may mean "I love the unborn," or it may mean "God hates murder." You will not know what a theist's motivation is until you ask.

Understanding Theism 101: NBC News political director Chuck Todd said (Zhao 2019) that Christians like Trump because they believe in fairy tales. Roughly 77 percent of the world's population subscribes to the idea of a God or gods (Harper 2012). Most of us draw a distinct line between our religious beliefs and, say, the Easter Bunny. I think Chuck's thesis has all sorts of problems. Many of my favorite Christian friends have a sincere, deep aversion to Mr. Trump despite a belief in fairy tales. Also, Chuck showed a strong attachment to fairy tales in his own right when he thought Hillary had the 2016 thing locked up, but that is neither here nor there.

My primary issue with Chuck's dismissal of people of faith is that he arrogantly assumes our faith is completely baseless. What Mr. Todd is clearly saying is that people who believe in God are idiots. He means to say Christians are idiots, but he has lumped our Muslim and Jewish friends into the fairy tale mix. I wonder if he meant to do that?

As far as a baseless faith held by the weak-minded and mentally feeble is concerned, I have spent years trying to show that the belief in the supernatural is not a brainless Nestea plunge into an empty pool. I personally have reasons to believe that are supported by scientific method, reason, the authority of brilliant minds, empirical evidence, and even personal experience.

Understanding Theism 101: Practicing theists have good arguments for believing in God. We use all five of the basic methods of learning: (1) personal experience, (2) empirical evidence, (3) reason/logic, (4) authority, and (5) the scientific method. We often discuss proofs for God from ontological arguments from the nature of being or existence, epistemological arguments from the nature of reason, or ethical arguments from the nature of behavior.

We also do not really believe in "blind faith" the way many seem to understand it. Faith always has an object, and the better we know our faith-object, the more we can trust it. Faith helps us to act when there is a gap between what we see and what we trust will be.

Understanding Theism 101: Practicing theists sometimes take heat from other worldview adherents because of their belief in a personal God who is impossible to see. The sacred writings from all three major theistic religions reveal some common responses to this charge.

We agree that God is hidden. We think He is hidden from the natural world because He is beyond nature, supernatural, as it were. He is spirit and transcendent. We believe He is hidden intentionally, possibly to weed out the spiritually blind and to allow for free will. He could overwhelm us, but that would not be fair to us. He is hidden because of our behavior, as sin separates us from God. He is hidden from us providentially. It is in our best interest to seek Him over time, whether we understand it or not.

It is a little too simple to say the idea of a God who is hard to find makes that kind of God a stupid idea. That is a little like saying, "Why doesn't that parent just give their child whatever the child wants? That parent is cruel." Well, the parent understands and values something different from simply making their child happy.

Understanding Theism 101: Here are a few things practicing theists *do not* believe:

God is a wish-grantor: Many times people from different perspectives seem to think that we theists view God as something akin to a magic genie in the sky. That is a cartoon version of God and is only good for ad hominem attacks on theism.

God is easy to understand: Sometimes nontheists (not many of you, just the angry ones) will claim that theism is stupid because if God is so smart and powerful, why do His followers disagree on so much? With three major theistic religions and a minimum of 4,200 different sects, denominations, and offshoots, this seems like a good question (Adhererents.com 2015). Practicing theists, however, do not think it is easy to find God's will and plan. We say things like, "The ways of God are different from the ways of man," "His ways are above our ways," and "We cannot fathom the ways of God." *Fathom.* We use fathom to explain this. If that does not prove we struggle with finding His ways for us, nothing will.

God wants us to be happy: Practicing theists believe that God wants us to thrive in the area of personal peace. Happiness is a different thing.

God does not want us to be happy: This is the same thing, but the other side of the coin. Enjoy happiness while you have it, but do not strive for it. I always say that those who strive for happiness never attain it, but if you strive for character, happiness often catches you from behind.

Understanding Theism 101: For a practicing theist, faith is not blind, as some people suppose. All faith is placed in a faith-object, such as a chair, the red light on the other side of the stoplight, or God. The better we know our faith-object, the more freely we place our hope in our faith-object. For me, knowing God is a journey I began to live thirty-one years ago. Today, January 8, 2013, is my first day living that journey without my father. Some may see it as a crutch for a weak and closed mind, but to me it is the hope upon which I watched my father swing out into eternity, and right now, peace is a blessed thing.

Bye, Dad. I will miss you so much.

Understanding Theism 101: Practicing theists believe not only in a singular God, but also in a personal God. The three major strains of theism all believe in the same God, and we can all recognize Him as the God of Abraham. After Abraham the Muslims went their own way in understanding who God is, and after Christ Christians went a different route and left their Judaic heritage. When we say that we believe God is personal, we are saying He has personality and identity, and we can talk to and hear from Him. It oversimplifies the issue to say we should all see Him the same way. After all, some people in this world see me as their son, others see me as their father, and others see me as their counselor. Others see me as the irritating basketball parent in the stands.

Understanding Theism 101: A common criticism against biblical theism is generally phrased this way: Why would a loving God send billions of people to hell? Biblical theists do not believe God sends anyone to hell. We think people are going to hell by their own choice. We believe God saves us from hell through a "Save-ior," named Jesus. All theists believe in hell, and in each expression, hell is less of a place for bad people than it is a place for those who have willingly disconnected from God. If there really is a hell, I don't want to be there.

Understanding Theism 101: Practicing theists believe in God. This is obvious. God, for theists, is distinct in at least three ways: (1) God is personal, which means He has a personality and an identity. (2) God is intentional. He has plans and interests. (3) God is transcendent. He interacts with His creation. This is all quite different from the god or gods of the pantheistic worldview. In pantheism God is typically represented as a force, just like in Star Wars (Lucas 1977). He may be presented as a balance, such as yin and yang, or karma. He may even be a universal oneness, absorbed and absorbing everything, sort of like Star Trek's Borg (Hurley 1989).

Understanding Theism 101: Practicing theists believe that God is all-powerful. He can do anything. Nontheists often argue that if God is all-powerful, why do bad things happen, or why does He not make Himself more easily seen? He either must not be all-powerful, or else He is not loving. At the very least, He is disinterested in us. Bertrand Russell used these arguments in his famous essay "Why I Am Not a Christian" (1957).

Two points: First, theists believe that even though God is all-powerful, He must allow us to freely choose to acknowledge Him. Otherwise, we are nothing more than video-game characters in a rigged game. The slightest dose of God's revealed presence would overwhelm us. We could never freely choose Him. Our freedom of choice leads to evil. C. S. Lewis (Mere Christianity 1952, renewed 1980, 23) of Narnia fame once said that evil is nothing more than a corrupted good. God did not make evil, but He allows us to choose against Him. Oversimplistically, this might mean we take a good thing, like whole grains, overprocess them and eat them in too great a quantity, causing ourselves to become obese by our gluttony, get heart disease, and die at forty-one, leaving our eight-year-old fatherless. God could prevent that, but only by overwhelming our free will.

Second point: Even if God were a bad God, which I do not believe, just being mad at Him for that is not a reason to disbelieve in the supernatural. The "loving" trait is a descriptor of God that theists attach to His character. You must answer the God/no God question apart from His loving nature. *That* He exists is a separate issue from *how* He exists.

Understanding Theism 101: Practicing theists believe deeply in the concept of faith but take exception to the idea that God cannot be proven to exist. In fact, they believe there are many, many ways to prove the existence of God. It is fair to say that any proof offered can provoke a discussion of the validity of that proof. Somebody with a different view can make an argument that our proof is wrong or inconclusive. That is where faith comes in. At some point, we have to say that it is not ridiculous to conclude there is a God. It should be noted that our worldview informs us how and what to argue for and against when considering these proofs.

Take, for instance, Thomas Aquinas's (The Summa Theologica of Saint Thomas Aquinas, English Translation 1948) second of his five proofs: the argument from efficient cause. In a nutshell, Aquinas is saying that every action is caused by another action, and moving backwards, there must be an uncaused first action. Aquinas calls this "uncaused cause" God. There may be many arguments against his conclusion, and some think it is simplistic. Yet, in every other situation, the application of Occam's razor is applauded. Others think it is too complex. It must be admitted, even by naturalistic atheists, that their own answer to the question of where stuff came from is only a theory. And that theory has more intellectual holes than they would often like to admit. Have you ever seen the photo of Einstein looking through the Hubble Telescope? He is puzzling over a great conundrum. He knew what the problem was. The universe is expanding away from a center point that happens to be in the neighborhood in which we live. This is awfully coincidental for a big bang. It may be a leap of faith to accept the supernatural proposition that God exists, but it is not intellectual suicide .

Understanding Theism 101: Hard work aside, practicing theists do not really believe in luck. Luck is more for atheists, who believe that events occur at the same statistical rates for everyone, and those who have more or less beneficial circumstances may be called lucky or unlucky. Theists tend to believe more in fortune. The fortunate or the less fortunate are often defined by theists as either blessed or cursed. What one theist takes as a blessing, another might take as a curse. It is often perspective and theology that are argued within the theistic camps on this point. For instance, some biblical theists think wealth is a sign of God's blessing. Others think wealth is a lie, and peace is where it is at. The bottom line is that theists believe God is involved in our circumstances, good and bad, and usually for reasons we can't currently see.

Understanding Theism 101: One of the ways theism differs from deism is clarified in how we answer the God/no god question. We both answer, "God, but..." As Pee-wee Herman says, "Everyone has a big but" (Ruebens 1985) A theist says God is personal and has both identity and personality. He is intentional in that He is creative and wills that things are done. He is transcendent, interacting with His creation. Deists are usually in agreement on the first two factors, but on the third, transcendence, a deist believes that either God chooses not to relate or is incapable of interfering with His creation. It is sort of like He pushed the "on" button and left.

Pantheists, on the other hand, dig the transcendence thing but do not believe God is personal. They see God more as an ultimate source, or force, as in "trust the Force, Luke." Often pantheists take on polytheistic traits and look to many "small *g*" gods, but those gods are always subject to the Brahman or the Samsara or something like that. It seems to me that Buddhism is the place where former theists and former atheists like to hold hands. It is spiritual, but there is no personal God.

Understanding Theism 101: Practicing theists often forget just how amazing their belief system must appear to those who do not hold their worldview. To believe so wholeheartedly in a God that cannot be seen is crazy-talk to those who cannot see. Biblical theists raise the ante. We add a God who became man and dwelt in the world. Then we add that God was killed and rose again. Then we add that this same God has made a way to dwell within us *and* that He wants us to go into the world and demonstrate His love. This is quite amazing. Why are we surprised when a billboard pops up telling us we are stupid? This is absolutely nuts to those who do not share our worldview.

I often say that theism is the only worldview that requires its adherents to convince others to accept their position. This is because we believe the bridge is out. An atheist or freethinker has no reason to convince a theist that he or she is wrong from the perspective of their worldview. I am thinking this position might have a caveat. They might think we are harming them somehow, and certainly they may be offended by our judgmentalism. Many of us are so bad at living the ideal life of theistic zeal that the rest of the world just needs us to shut up. So they fight back. My advice for biblical theists, the only ones I can advise, is to offer more heart, less attack (Needtobreathe 2014).

Understanding Theism 101: I want to do a miniseries on biblical theists and some of the biggest misconceptions they have about God. Let me tell you where this comes from. This week I got a call from a college student whom I had never met. She was referred to me by another student I barely know, but I was the pastor whose number she had. This young lady's first question floored me: "Will I go to hell if I commit suicide?" Oh my!

I think God spoke to my heart and my brain actually paid attention. There were so many places I could have started. I could have offered theology lessons or called 911. I could have told her that Jesus saves or told her that I loved her even though I had never met her. Instead, I asked her, "Would you go to hell if you died in a car accident tonight?" It was quiet for a moment, and then while she was softly crying, she told me that my question changed everything. We eventually met and had a serious conversation about why she was contemplating suicide, but we really got to work on the idea that God loved her deeply, no matter how much shame and hopelessness she had for herself. She walked away from our meeting with a new resolve and a list of choices that were designed to help her. One of those choices included dropping out of school and moving back home to parents who she found were ready to support her when she expected nothing but condemnation.

There are a lot of things to take from this story, but the one I want my theistic friends to understand is this: God does not hate anybody for what they do, believe, or think about themselves. He does not hate those with gender-identity concerns, or alcoholics, or Raider fans. Our sacred text says God loved everyone so much that He gave His Son to die on a cross to set us free from guilt and condemnation.

Of course, there is a catch, but we have always known about that. We must give ourselves over to His will. He will make us right.

Understanding Theism 101: Let's continue with this miniseries about misconceptions about God. This one came up in one of the recent discussions we had about morality and ethics in one of my classes at Colorado Christian University. The statement we are challenging is that theists should not expect the nature of God to stay static; He changes over time and expects our moral standards to change as well. Our Scriptures clearly have such stalwarts as Moses, David, Malachi, Jesus, and Paul telling us that this is not true because God does not change.

What does change for theists are values and cultures, and we often want to change with them. I believe we should all adapt to certain new realities, but we should not ever go against the revealed text. Theists have an obligation to verify cultural expectations according to Scripture, not to dismiss Scripture because the culture invalidates it. Cultures have always existed and always will. The same cultures we currently castigate for being archaic were once considered to be cutting edge. Just because the current culture deems something to be correct does not mean a thing. Theists might know this better than anybody.

This is especially difficult in this day and age because it does not take much talk about sexual, gender, and marriage norms according to the Bible to get yourself a free "bigot in the house" T-shirt.

Understanding Theism 101: I heard this next misconception about God while visiting with one of my homeless friends in the park across the street. I don't know if he really believes it, but I am sure many of us do. He said the reason he is homeless is because he is being punished by God for being a bad child to his parents.

It is easy to see that he is homeless because he does not work, but that obvious judgment aside, I think a lot of us can relate to this idea that God is pretty much a vindictive S.O.B. It is true that God looks at suffering in a less than sympathetic way, but we believe that is because He sees the future much more clearly than we do and is aware that suffering produces strength and growth in our lives. God also tells us that He knows we will have trouble in this world, but to take heart for He has overcome the world.

Last but not least, if my buddy had a job, he wouldn't have to be homeless. Bad things do happen to good people, but I bet about 85 percent of our suffering is due to our own stupid selves. Oh, and do not be angry at me regarding my callousness toward my homeless friend; I've bought him more lunches than you have!

Understanding Theism 101: Well, there has been lots of feedback on these posts. I am compelled to balance out the first of these misconception posts, where I took the position that God does not hate anybody. Though nobody disagreed with that in general, there was pushback saying that God will pass judgment on all of us. The misconception is that God will not pass judgment on me or anyone else.

It is true that God will indeed pass judgment. Biblical theists struggle with Matthew's message from the mouth of Jesus that there will be a day when He will separate the sheep and the goats (Matthew 25). This is barnyard talk for heaven and hell. Where I differ from some of the comments about the nature of God is in this: I do not believe that biblical theism supports the concept that God sends people to hell for anything. I believe we go to hell on our own accord. It is our choice from the beginning. God has done the opposite of sending us to hell; He has provided a way for us not to go. It was a very expensive way, at that. When Jesus judges us in Matthew 25, He is simply announcing the decision that we have made all along.

So, in the end, there will be a judgment by God, but He will not judge us according to what He has decided. He will judge us according to what *we* have decided. Bronco fan, Bronco fan, Raider fan, Bronco fan, and on it goes.

Understanding Theism 101: I got this next thought from a conversation on campus with a bunch of Christian students who were discussing an anti-alcohol diatribe called *Hand Me a Dr. Pepper, Please* (Shuler 2010). This misconception is that God wants to mess up our fun.

Well, this is partly true, that is for sure. There are many things that are fun that God does not want us doing. I don't think that it is without plenty of caveat. Every single thing that could be called a sin is some form of a ruined good. Theists do not believe God created any evil. If we reduce this a bit, we come to a place that tells us God wants us to enjoy things. He wants us to have fun within the right framework. Sex is fun even when you are no good at it, but it is not good in God's eyes for you or anybody else if it is not practiced within the right context. God gives instruction for that context. Jokes are fun, but God tells us not to harm others with our words or to be coarse, so there are lots of situations where God wants to ruin some fun. When it is in the right place and time and can encourage or build others up, those are the times when that fun is allowed.

I hate this one because my fun might be ruined, too, if I just pay a little more attention. We biblical theists think the Holy Spirit cools our jets for our own good.

Understanding Theism 101: I will be brief with these next misconceptions about the nature of God:

> God is not a Republican.
> God is not a Democrat.
> God is not a Libertarian.
> God is not a conservative.

God is not a liberal.

God is not an American.

God is not white.

God is not black.

God is not any other color.

God is not a Bronco fan, so quit praying for wins.

God is not a Raider fan, so quit blaming Him when we lose.

God is not a man, except for one brief exception.

God is not a woman.

God is not a Baptist.

God is not a Methodist.

God is not a Catholic.

God is not any other religion or denomination.

God is not a capitalist.

God is not a socialist.

Understanding Theism 101: Theists of all stripes believe that the Creator is absolutely good and uncorrupted, and that He wants those who follow Him to be good as well. In every form of monotheism, God has made His thoughts about this known. The way He has done this throughout the theistic religions may include His revealed, unalterable directives through written communication. It may be revealed in many ways and is available to be known in different details by individuals, which means we believe He may lead individuals in certain ways. Islam is on the front of that spectrum, and biblical Christianity is close to the other end. In Islam, nobody will tell their friends that Allah is leading them to reach out to and be inclusive of the LGBTQ+ crowd. In biblical theism, this happens all the time, and the followers must sort through what this will mean. The rigidity of Islam may be seen as either a blessing or a curse, just as the fluidity of Christianity may be seen as one or the other as well.

Understanding Theism 101: Theists believe God has given direction about how humankind should operate. Religion may be described as a system in which a group of common believers operate in their pursuit of following God. When you put those two sentences together, you create thousands of bounded circles of a few people who believe the same general thing. If you give them long enough and let them start talking, the circles will break into smaller and smaller groups, often getting fractionalized all the way down to the last person. Religions and denominations are agreements by religious people that they will stick to some core principles and stay away from the edges in order to stay united. There is always a tension, though.

Chapter 5

Theism and the Supernatural

The next of our defining questions as we further explain the theistic worldview is, Do you believe in the supernatural? Yes. God is beyond nature, and so is the spiritual world and the afterlife.

Understanding Theism 101: Practicing theists believe in miracles. Sometimes we believe so strongly in them that we beg for them or see them where they have not really happened. But we believe in them, and the reason we believe in small miracles, such as the $126 we got when we needed $126, or Grandma's cancer going into remission, is because we believe in the big miracle—God outside of nature.

Stephen Hawking's incredibly disappointing *The Grand Design* (2010) is a philosophy book that begins with Hawking's pompous claim of the death of philosophy. One of his many nonscientific and philosophical conclusions is that since we know the laws of nature, miracles are impossible. Theists have long enjoyed C. S. Lewis's metaphor of the dresser drawer. He said that if he put $1,000 in the drawer one week, $2,000 the next, and $1,000 again the next week, the laws of arithmetic would allow him to conclude that that he would find $4,000 in the drawer. But if he only finds $1,000, it would be silly to conclude that the laws of arithmetic had been broken. It would be more likely that the laws of the state were broken by a thief. Lewis says that the one thing we cannot do is to deny the existence of the thief based upon the laws of arithmetic. On the contrary, he says, "It is the normal working of those laws that have exposed the existence and workings of the thief" (C. S. Lewis, Miracles 1974-reprint).

Such do theists believe regarding God and the laws of nature. We see God, in a large part, because of the evidence that is beyond nature's easy explanations.

Understanding Theism 101: Practicing theists ask God for help and guidance. We are often accused of mistaking coincidence for Providence.

Two points: First, it takes both a request and a result to make a coincidence. It is only a coincidence because we have taken the time to ask! Second, practicing theists are extremely far from the "genie in the sky" God that is a popular perception from those with differing worldviews. In biblical theism, for instance, our prayers are only answered in the affirmative when we get to that place where Jesus would sign off on our requests before He sends them on to God. Basically, the key is to be in tune with God to such a degree that we are praying for His will to be done, regardless of what we want. The only surefire motivation for any prayer request is that what we are asking for will somehow bring glory to God. For instance, when we pray for a dying parent, we must admit that God might be more glorified in how we deal with our loss.

Understanding Theism 101: Many modern "theists" have given up on the idea that there is anything in the realm of supernatural thought that should have any weight upon serious theology. A pastor friend of mine sincerely expressed that her church does not embrace any of the mythologies of Christianity, such as prayer, fasting, virgin births, or resurrected gods. This is not authentic theism. It is essentially humanism, where individual people do their best to become as good and loving as they possibly can.

Understanding Theism 101: Theists do science, but scientists rarely do theism. Science is defined as "the systematic study of the structure and behavior of the physical and natural world through observation, experimentation, and the testing of theories against the evidence obtained" (Definition of science in English 2016). This definition is typical of several that I looked at today. In each case, the distinction is made that science is a study of the natural world, and this stands to exclude anything beyond the natural. Science studies normal natural, but not supernatural. Theists are aware that science is not going to find God in the natural world because when God enters the natural, He breaks the rules, like that time Jesus was born, and died and was buried and rose from the dead. Science says that people can't rise from the dead, so it didn't happen. We theists know that people can't rise from the dead—we're not idiots. That's why we are so surprised about that time Jesus rose from the dead.

Nothing about this is odd or surprising. I point it out just because it is worth understanding that there is a strong apples-and-oranges thing going on in the world.

By the way, 36 percent of scientists in the United States have "no doubt that God exists" (Ecklund 2010). That is above the 29 percent of Americans in general who have no doubt that God exists (Ibid.).

Understanding Theism 101: Many "theists" believe in ghosts or spirits or omens or Ouija boards or whatever.

Nontheists might think theists need to figure out that declaring some supernatural ideas as myths and others as truth is a little disingenuous. So, we don't believe in the Easter Bunny, but we do believe that guy who was dead is not dead anymore? Yep.

Practicing theists are obligated to discern between myths and amazing supernatural conditions they consider to be real. A good piece of advice came out of a 1980s song: "If the Bible doesn't back it, it seems quite clear that it must have been the devil that whispered in your ear" (Taylor, Guilty by Association 1984). There is, according to biblical theism, a supernatural realm. It is occupied by God. He references angels and demons. That is a lot, but there is nothing beyond that. Anything else is nothing but Easter Bunnies. This includes the idea that our deceased family and friends are watching down over us from heaven. As much as I wish that were true, it is not supported biblically. The biblical explanation is much closer to the idea that when we pass out of time, we step into eternity. I believe that when I die and run across my long-dead grandfather, he is going to be a new arrival also. This makes me feel better, because the last thing I would want is for him to have been a helpless observer over the lives of myself and my sixty-three cousins over all these years. I do believe that it is fine to remember somebody with fondness during the best moments of our lives, or to strive to maintain the legacies of good people.

Theists would be wise to chill on the ghosts and things. None of our sacred texts support those ideas without being stretched out of shape.

Understanding Theism 101: There is a word that lives on the borders between the natural and the supernatural. *Metaphysics* is a word for philosophers, and it is basically a discussion of abstract theories about real things like love, beauty, justice, and the like.

Theists embrace these metaphysical concepts because we feel they provide glimpses into the supernatural. Science cannot measure in a laboratory something like love, but it can measure chemical reactions to pictures of beautiful women, babies, and spouses.

How do I love thee? Let me count the ways. First, my dopamine levels go through the roof when you wear that red dress. What a buzzkill.

Natural science gives way to behavioral science, which gives way to psychology, which is turning natural science standards into a joke these days. All of a sudden, we live in a world where science can't figure how many restrooms are needed, while the supernaturally abstract metaphysical theists are still insisting that the science is settled on the who-goes-into-which-restroom debate.

Understanding Theism 101: Authentic theists begin with the presupposition that God exists. We believe that He exists outside of nature. He is capable of interacting with nature, including things like the weather, parking spaces, cancer, and pregnancies. For our friends who do not believe there is anything beyond nature, this looks like lunacy. Some theists who have a diminished or weak capacity for faith know they should believe in such things, yet they find themselves doubting that the God in which they hope is listening, or even there at all.

There are several reasons why theists lose faith. Biblical theism addresses this question directly: you pray and you ask, but you get nothing (James 4:1-4). Two reasons are offered. The first is that we really don't even ask. We give up on our hope in the God beyond nature. Instead of praying to God, many biblical theists now pray to social media: "Grandma's in the hospital! Prayers needed!" My guess is that the person who posts these sorts of requests does not really get into a posture of prayer to seek God. They do very little beyond sharing their need and wishing for the best. The second reason we do not get what we ask for is that we ask with wrong motives. The short answer to this for the biblical theist is to pray for anything that we know Jesus would sign off on.

By the way, He signs off on things that bring glory to His Father (John 17:4).

Understanding Theism 101: Yesterday's post demands a little more thought. Theists believe God desires to be glorified. The fact that the creator of the universe would reach into the created makes Him worthy of being held in esteem. When we pray to a God who is beyond the natural, we are obligated to recognize that He has made a way for us to connect.

Most people do not understand what is happening when a theist prays. It seems like it is often perceived by nontheists as something akin to hope or wishing. In reality theists pray much more conversationally than might be thought. We do not simply ask for things like money, parking spaces, and girlfriends. Theists desperately seek God's guidance and direction. We spend lots of time in prayer simply being grateful for friends, family, and good things. We talk to God about almost anything that a loving married couple might talk about with each other.

Mature, practicing theists also do one other thing in prayer that nontheists may not know about: they listen. God doesn't speak to many of us in an audible voice. Even the best of us gets worried when one of our buddies tells us, "God told me something."..."Uh, I gotta go."

No, we just talk to God for a while, and then we close our trap and wait for that transcendent moment where we feel rather than hear the whisper of God moving us away from anxiety and toward peace if we will simply follow. It is sweet when it happens. It feels as real as anything.

Understanding Theism 101: A big word in the world of theism is *spirituality*. Spirituality is generally defined as being concerned with the human soul or spirit, rather than being primarily concerned with material or physical interests. Theists believe that people have an immeasurable part of themselves that they are not only intrinsically aware of, but that this spirit is key to connecting with things beyond nature, beyond their reality. It is a spiritual connection between ourselves and the God we worship. The important word in describing this ethereal state is *transcendence*. Literally, it is the act of interacting with the supernatural.

Folks from a lot of different worldviews embrace the spiritual, and even naturalists can have spiritual moments while watching a sunset or meditating upon a child's innocent beauty. But for most worldviews, those thoughts of transcendence usually top out at moments of profound recognition of the wonder of life or some sort of physical ecstasy. Religious worldviews tend to hold spiritual experiences as real encounters with the supernatural. For theists, those real experiences are connections with God.

Theists are wary of false spiritualities. We biblical theists, for instance, sometimes feel that the euphoria caused by dimmed lights and growing drumbeats may cause us to be faked out, so some of us don't like Christian music that is too good. "That's not Jesus! That's just a well-played D minor!"

Understanding Theism 101: One way that theists differ from pantheists in a general sense is in how they meditate. Meditation is an important part of transcendence. It is an effort to bring our minds into alignment with spiritual truths or realities.

Pantheists include some large world religions such as Taoism and Hinduism. Meditation in these traditions usually involves the emptying of the mind in an effort to connect with a supernatural essence of the universe. For theists, meditation is a spiritual discipline that involves contemplation, usually upon Scripture or the character or nature of God.

Understanding Theism 101: Biblical theists have a lot of built-in interactions with the supernatural within their day-to-day walk of faith. This walk of faith is described in the Bible as being distinct from walking by sight.

Sight represents the natural world, and faith represents the connection with the supernatural world.

We are often accused of having blind faith. Blind faith is meant to convey the idea that we are walking in the dark with nothing but luck to keep us from tripping stupidly over the facts that others can clearly see. But that is not how blind people generally walk. I know blind people who can move with complete freedom around their homes, and to lesser degrees can move unencumbered around neighborhoods and familiar spaces, and even unfamiliar locations can be managed with a few aids, such as sounds and white sticks.

Faith is not blind in the sense that we are completely lost. Faith is blind in the sense that because we are moving in the supernatural world as natural beings, our movement is encumbered with the need to become aware. We have aids to help us as well. Included among these helps are a growing knowledge of our faith-object, which is God, the confidence that familiarity brings, and our own version of a white stick, the Bible.

So, yes, theists really believe that they can have moments of transcending the natural and entering the supernatural.

Understanding Theism 101: My last post provoked a lot of conversation, especially about the different ways that we interact with the supernatural as biblical theists. I thought I would comment briefly on some of these interactions.

Theists believe that we experience miracles. A miracle is an event within the natural world that was caused by an actor from the world beyond nature. We believe that God has the power as the creator and sustainer of the universe to reach in and make adjustments to the cosmos, especially upon the requests of His followers. We are all over the map on how often this happens and what it looks like when it happens. Some feel that calling anything miraculous without really searching the cause could be dangerous. If theists call every coincidence a miracle, they will have trouble fighting back against the very good question, Why doesn't God heal amputees? On the other hand, giving up on miracles altogether seems to challenge our basic belief in the strength, power, and love of God.

Biblical theists believe in supernatural healing. This could be called a miracle, but the Bible just refers to healings as its own category of the supernatural work of God. I have been around when seemingly unexplained things happened regarding the health of someone who was being prayed for in specific ways. I will be honest; I don't know how my naturalistic friends respond when miracles happen to them. I believe God does perform miracles on occasion for those who do not believe. I think they just go with the flow.

There is an interaction with the supernatural that biblical theists call "words of knowledge." These are messages that contain real information that could not be known in any natural way. I have experienced warnings from a woman to be ready to help a young mother in the coming days because she would be entering into a great struggle, only to find out less than twenty-four hours later that her young husband was killed in a work accident. How did this woman know? She said she was simply praying and God told her the young woman was going to be alone with her children. It does not happen a lot, but I have seen it enough that I can't just throw it aside as coincidence.

Biblical theists believe they can have encounters with supernatural beings from time to time. Biblical theists believe that other than God, this realm is occupied by angels and demons only—no ghosts. I have experienced these interactions. Could they be explained away? Probably, but they stand out among the most vivid memories I have, even after more than forty years in one case. I have had encounters with both the dark side and the side of the light. We often talk about things such as spiritual warfare.

Biblical theists believe that God can break the wall between the supernatural and the natural as they worship, and things happen such as speaking in tongues. Some people might prophesy, which means making predictions about events. Some churches feature healing events. I'm not as familiar with these, and even God warns us that these things need to be checked against reality. But it is a thing, and a weekly thing for some of my theistic friends.

Just imagine what our naturalistic friends might think when they read this!

Understanding Theism 101: Practicing theists do a thing we call worship. Worship is different from appreciation. I think anybody can look at the right sunrise on the right lake at the right time of year and recognize there is a transcendent experience, even if it is just with the natural world. Worship is different in that theists target their appreciation of the good and beautiful by directing their gratitude towards the Creator. It is even a step beyond that because we see God as not only the Creator, but as a sustainer. In even one more step, worship acknowledges that the beauty of that sunset is not just an accident of nature and psychology, but a loving gift from Father to child.

All of this is an active connection for the theist between the natural world and the supernatural. As weird as it is that we believe this, it is remarkably deeply ingrained into our experience. Science calls it simple euphoria. We believe we are meeting God.

Chapter 6

Theism and the Natural World

Here is the fourth question in which our answer further defines the worldview of theism: where do you think stuff came from? Theists believe that God made everything in the natural world from scratch. It is a necessary requirement for the creator of nature to be outside of nature, which is the exact opposite of the big bang.

Understanding theism 101: Practicing theists believe in the supernatural. This is why theists and atheists have a hard time being friends whenever one or the other makes a comment about anything beyond nature, like God. The scientific-type atheists are called naturalists not because they love the environment, but because they believe in natural law. Practicing theists do not believe in everything supernatural, just that certain aspects of reality, the God stuff, is not scientifically measurable.

This leads me to mention two things that I find interesting about naturalistic atheism: First, for a naturalist, the scientific method is the ultimate way to obtain reliable knowledge about life, the universe, and the big questions. Scientific method requires two things, absolute control in the study and repeatability. According to my college textbook on research design, absolute control is impossible to attain. That is why the thesis/antithesis/synthesis/thesis model of research is always refining the search for the truth. You do a study, I do a counter-study, and someone else counters mine, and so on. I love the scientific method. I rely on it in many ways, but not only does it never get to the truth, but it often hits dead ends and needs to begin again. That is why we have commercials for class-action lawsuits if you once took some medicine for something that might make you die from something else. Theists are not convinced that the scientific method is the end of the discussion.

Second, and more fun, naturalistic atheists like Sheldon Cooper and friends, provide the television image of the worldview. And these guys love superheroes. *The Big Bang Theory* (Lorre and Prady 2007) is the literary response to Jack London's *Call of the Wild* (1903, republished 1982). Instead of Buck reaching for his evolutionary ancestry, Sheldon is hearing his call from the comic bookstore to connect with the supernatural. And that, my friends, is a great observation. Score one for Darrin.

Understanding Theism 101: Theists do not deny the natural world. We stub our toes on it all the time. Some adherents of other worldviews do deny the reality of the natural world. That is why they sleep on beds of nails and walk across burning coals.

Understanding Theism 101: Theists and naturalistic atheists remind me of Trump and Biden supporters trying to have a decent Thanksgiving meal together. We get along fine until somebody says something.

There is a bit of a philosophical debate among the scientists and the theologians about where the debate about the nature of reality actually begins. One camp says that we are fundamentally disagreeing about the nature of God versus no god. The other camp feels that we are fundamentally talking about the difference between being a naturalist versus an anti-naturalist. Do theists arrive at a belief in God because they are against the thought that every phenomenon can essentially be explained through laws of nature? Do naturalists simply never arrive at God because they do not have a launching pad from the flat ground of naturalism? Do theists distrust nature as a complete explanation because they float from the presupposition that there is a God? Do naturalists drift from the beginning point of there is no God and slowly arrive at hardcore atheism? Of the four questions, the last one is the least likely.

Many thoughtful naturalists claim atheism is not a worldview, because it would be a view springing from a non-starting point. This makes sense to me. This is why I usually use the term *naturalistic atheist*. It would be fair to leave atheism out of the identity. The reason I don't do that in the posts is because naturalists are very different from theists and polytheists and pantheists and panentheists. It is a real distinction that observes a legitimate boundary between ideas.

Understanding Theism 101: Naturalistic atheists often define theists as anti-naturalists. This is okay because theists define naturalists as atheists. I think in each case, we are attempting to move the conversation to a common ground that barely exists. In fact, the only common ground we have is that we each recognize the broad land between our ideologies.

Let's consider the claim for a moment. Are theists anti-naturalists? Not in the true sense of the word. Theists believe in nature and laws of nature. If I crack my barefooted toe into a solid piece of nature called a rock, I most definitely believe that nature is real. A side note: Some pantheistic and panentheistic religions would deny the rock is real, and they would deny the pain, and they would deny the doctor's opinion that nature can be as hard as a rock.

The word that better fits traditional theistic thinking regarding nature would be *dualism*. Dualism is the division of something conceptually into two opposed or contrasted aspects, or a state of being divided. To a naturalist, this may be even crazier than simply denying nature altogether. Theists believe that God created all material and arranged it in an order that is made consistent through natural laws. We believe God is revealed through the natural world. Biblical theism puts the weight of knowing that there is a God upon those who have never been told there is a God by saying that with our own eyes we can see His glory in the heavens and the earth. A friend of mine was a rockhound—he loved everything geological. For him, every hike through a desert was a chance to meet God.

Understanding Theism 101: Theists have created a lot of bad press for themselves when it comes to their interaction with nature. Only in recent years have we begun to champion environmental concerns. I'm glad to see this shift, along with greater care for animals.

The Qur'an teaches Islamic theists not to waste the abundance of the earth or to squander its resources. In Judaic theism, rules are so precise as to even account for when a city has been under siege for a long time, the invaders are not to destroy the fruit trees, but to care for and protect them.

The Bible encourages Christians to recognize they have been given a trust over which they are to stand as stewards, or caretakers, of the natural world.

Understanding Theism 101: Theists really do not like teenage girls screaming at them about global warming and the end of life as we know it. I don't think anybody likes teenage girls screaming at them about anything. It is a silly way to try to change somebody's mind.

I can certainly see that we who are living in the richest parts of the world have earned the right to be put in our place on this issue. Oftentimes the wonderful theistic expectation that we assume a role of caretaking of the environment is traded in for a simple desire to manage and consume its resources. I am encouraged by the number of people in my camp of biblical theists who are embracing their love of nature by responsibly promoting best practices in engaging with the environment.

Perhaps noisy teenagers have helped us to reconnect. We should have figured it out on our own.

Understanding Theism 101: Theists are not very connected to global warming and environmental change issues. The bumper stickers on our cars are "Love Everyone" and "God Created Fracking."

There is a theistically derived reality involving God and the natural world that explains this lack of concern. It does not explain the lack of manners in expressing the lack of concern. That is on us. Theists are simply not going to be afraid of the world ending unless God wants it to end. We believe the world is in decay, and that one day, when God calls the note due, everything that is messed up will be made right.

I believe that one of the ten best things theists can do to bring credence to their worldview is to engage as a non-anxious presence regarding the environment. One part of this would be that we reflect our confidence and faith that everything will, in the end, be all right. The other is that we refrain from creating anxiety in the lives of others who are deeply and reasonably concerned about these issues. That is as simple to begin as to stop making fun of recycling.

Understanding Theism 101: Theists may be skeptical of too much ecological fervor. I read an essay called "Green Guilt" (Asma 2010) today. The writer had no grudge against thinking green, but he was appalled at his six-year-old child's evangelistic fervor and terror that such things as running water while brushing teeth were going to ruin the earth.

We can get almost all we need to understand the writer's point from the title of his essay. Asma was well-measured but very dismayed that the religious framework his child was choosing was as an environmentalist. It had all the best parts of any good religion. There was evangelism to a point of view, punishment with hell, atonement, redemption, and most of all, guilt.

Theists do worry that important causes can become primary religious fervor. When the second-best thing becomes the greatest enemy to the best thing, we must be very careful not to throw the baby out with the polluted bathwater.

Understanding Theism 101: Theists tend to battle with environmentalists, especially the ones who seek to give equal value to every created thing. There are serious environmentalists who believe that plants, bugs, and animals are on equal par with humans. Theists reject this almost without exception.

There is a growing movement among theists, especially biblical theists, to be more compassionate, especially regarding animals. The Bible is revolutionary in its message to care for animals, and biblical theists are making strides by demanding compassionate change in the treatment of domestic pets and the animals raised for food production. Many theists are joining the ranks of the once-maligned vegetarian crowd.

But if you want to make a theist angry, tell them that a pet is as important as a human.

Understanding Theism 101: Theists are encouraged by their Scriptures to let various laws of nature teach supernatural truths. God uses our understanding of the way things are to inform us of the way things could be. For instance, He encourages us to be fair-minded when we remember that the rains fall on the fields of both the righteous and the unrighteous. He teaches us about purity by reminding us that the Word of God washes us like running water. He uses deep-rooted trees to illustrate unshakable ground for those who are disciplined to study His Scriptures.

One of my favorite biblical uses of nature to teach and inspire us toward supernatural truth is from the sixth chapter of Galatians. Paul encourages the Galatian people to remember three laws of the harvest: (1) We reap what we sow. If we sow apple seeds, we will produce apples. (2) We reap more than we sow. A handful of seed can produce bushels of produce. (3) We reap later than we sow. It takes a while for the crop to grow, but patience will produce the reward.

All of this is true for apple trees, but it is true as well for my home. If I want peace in my home, I should sow seeds of peace. Seeds of peace look insignificant because seeds are tiny, like small sentences here and there along with hugs and encouragement. Later, when my kids are grown, there will be a harvest of peace. If I am not careful, though, and sow seeds of discord by speaking insulting words and giving angry looks for the slightest failure, well, that crop grows as it was planted.

Understanding Theism 101: Theists believe God created the cosmos ex nihilo. That little phrase is Latin for "out of nothing." I will admit I could have said that we believe God created the cosmos out of nothing and that would have been easier, but you must admit that the way I said it made me sound smarter.

But it is true. We believe that God got His own dirt, and that He created the cosmos from nothing. We believe He spoke the cosmos into existence, and that it operates with a detailed and uniform sense of purpose through the entirety of natural laws. We believe He set the laws of cause and effect into place from this first uncaused action. We believe we exist in an open system where we might impact lives and matter by our impulses, which can exist via free will.

Chapter 7

Theism and the Nature of Time

The next of our defining questions is, What do you believe about the nature of time? Theists believe there was a beginning of time and will be an end. Eternity exists outside of time.

Understanding Theism 101: Biblical theists start with the beginning and end with the ending. Our story is the story of existing within the framework of time. This is why practicing theists do not believe in reincarnation. We simply have no instruction within our sacred texts that would suggest we can bounce around upon the timeline. Also, everyone who believes in reincarnation thinks they were once Cleopatra. She must have been one crazy lady.

Understanding Theism 101: Theists believe God exists outside of time. We believe time began when the already-existent God did the, "In the beginning, God..." thing. We believe that a real part of His nature is that He is omnipresent, which means He is everywhere, but also "everywhen." Everywhen is a word we never use because we are living *in* time.

One of the most comforting things about this belief is that it gives us confidence in the never-changing nature of God. We don't have to worry that a different, less-evolved version of God was running things during the 1960's or the Dark Ages or during Trump's presidency. Moses got a straight answer from God on this issue when he was going to speak to Pharoah. He asked God, "Who should I say sent me with this message?" and God answered, "Say I AM sent you." This is more than a clever gag to puzzle Pharoah. This is God declaring an ultimate reality. He does not have "was" or "will be" in His story. He is always ever present, and He sees the timeline of history and every moment spread out like a...like a...You know, I can't think of an analogy!

CRUISING THROUGH LIFE AT 60 MINUTES PER HOUR

Understanding Theism 101: For theists, time is a created thing that did not exist before God created the universe. Theists believe time is a tool that allows a word like *mortal* to have meaning. We live our lives in a mortal condition. The word expresses the idea that we are both subject to death and not divine in nature. That makes sense to people from a multitude of worldviews, especially the naturalistic views.

For the theist, however, there is a good reason for this gift of time, even though we fear death and resent non-godhood status. Time allows us an opportunity to exist within a framework where we can choose for or against our Creator. It is a blessing, but the mere nature of time and its greatest curse is that we run out of it. But we have a moment, and in that moment, we get to choose how we wish to launch into eternity, because we theists believe that death is when we escape the surly bonds of time.

Understanding Theism 101: All theists believe God created the universe; and in the midst of bringing order from the chaos, He separated the day from the night by spinning the earth around its axis, creating twenty-four-hour days, and putting our planet in motion around the sun, generating a seemingly never-ending number of seasons and years.

God added a twist to the spins and revolutions of time-making by putting a regular pause in the process on the seventh day. The Old Testament calls it a Sabbath, and it is designed to let us rest from the endless routines of life. The days and the years are set by the laws of nature, but the week is set by the creator God, trapped forever in the timeline of the ages as a gift of perpetual renewal. TGIF actually is an awesome thing!

Understanding Theism 101: Although generally unaware of it, theists basically believe that twenty-four hours is the exact perfect amount of time it takes to accomplish God's plan in our lives for one day. This means that if we are bored, it is because God has more for us to do within these particular twenty-four hours. If we are exhausted, it means we are doing more than God is asking. It means that if we are not accomplishing anything meaningful or moving toward our purpose, then we are not in tune with God's plan for us. Everything He means for us to do in the next twenty-four hours may be accomplished within those twenty-four hours. It might be hard, but if it is difficult, then that struggle helps us to grow stronger. It may sometimes be simple, and if it is, that simplicity should be known as a gift of peace. Theists pray for this. Biblical theists pray for God's will to be done within the context of taking daily bread. This is one reason why theists like to do the God-thing.

Understanding Theism 101: Time is defined as the progression of events from the past through the present into the future. This means that if a system is unchanging, it is timeless. That is why biblical theists totally dig the fact that God said His name is I AM.

Islam has a very similar idea from the Qur'an. There, Allah says not to waste time, for he *is* time.

Understanding Theism 101: One time in a Christian church, the pastor greeted the congregation with a friendly and encouraging, "Good morning, fellow time travelers!" Boy, I really liked that.

Understanding Theism 101: Biblical theists generally believe that God exists outside of time. I read a stupid article today on open theism that argued the contrary. One of the greatest things that emerges from our meta-narrative about God and time is the fact that God chose to invade time.

According to our sacred texts, God chose a point in time and a place on earth in which He planted a tiny baby who somehow contained the living essence of a divine God. Biblical theists believe that is the part of the triune nature of the holy God that we call the Son. Our texts tell us that He humbled Himself and gave up His divine nature and submitted, even to death, in order to invade our world in disguise (John 1, Philippians 2). He processed through time, eighteen years of His life contained in a single verse that says He grew in wisdom and in stature and in favor with God and men (Luke 2:52 NIV). He died as a sinless man, thus violating God's law of nature that says sin (any imperfection) causes death. When He rose from His grave alive, He reclaimed His godhood.

Biblical theists also believe that God's third part of the holy Trinity, the Spirit, has been given to us as a gift to guide and comfort us on our own journey through time. This distinguishes us from other theistic religions in a big way as the Son and the Holy Spirit each invade time.

Understanding Theism 101: In college I wrote a paper on William Faulkner's *The Sound and the Fury* (1929). The teacher commented on one of my references, saying that this was his favorite reference he had ever read in any paper on this wonderful novel about time. The reference I used was this: "Like a watch still ticking on a dead man's wrist, tick away. . ." (Jim Morrison's Grave, Taylor 1987). Theists believe that when we pass, we pass out of time.

Understanding Theism 101: For most folks, the passage of time is a chance to grow smarter and wiser and less dependent upon the necessity of God. For practicing theists, we believe that time allows us an opportunity to trust God and to rest more and more in our dependence upon Him.

Understanding Theism 101: I once read an amazing book by the theistic scholar-rabbi A. J. Heschel in which he stated that the history of Judaism is a history of time (God in Search of Man 1955). Heschel believed that contrary to the deities of other religions that were always marked by places or things, the God of Israel spoke to His created through a series of events and people marked out over time. This is absolutely wonderful.

Understanding Theism 101: Philosophical theists of all three major religions love to argue about the nature of God and time. The two extremes of the argument are either that God is timeless or that He is temporal. There is a lot of ground in between.

The timeless argument suggests that God does not pass through the events of time in succession, that He is above all of that and has a view of 1015 BC that is as clear as the view of AD 2093. The temporal view is that He is passing through time with us in a succession of moments. In biblical theology, this argument is huge for Reformed/not Reformed thinkers. But that is for a different book than Understanding Theism 101.

Thinking that God is temporal diminishes His divinity, in my mind. It opens the door for us to interpret God in the context of modern sensibilities and thus diminishes confidence in our sacred writings that would make them appear to be old-fashioned.

Understanding Theism 101: Theists have some interesting thinking regarding time and their bodies. We believe that God intentionally chose a point in time into which to insert us into the world, and at that point, we became slaves to the ticking clock. We cannot do some things because we are not old enough, and we cannot do other things because we are too dang old. Trapped inside this time-travel suit we call a body, our timeless soul longs for freedom.

Understanding Theism 101: Theists believe that human beings exist within time, not only moving from moment to moment, but existing within a series of moments. This is an idea that has been referred to as "a community of you" (J. B. Peterson 2021, 51). Every moment of my life offers a chance to make a decision that "future me" is either going to enjoy or pay for. When I eat Mexican food late at night, future me is going to experience the heartburn. I was discussing this with a friend who said that the eighteen-year-old who was president of his community of you forty years ago was still impacting his life in negative ways today.

This metaphysical time conversation is something that almost everyone could relate to if they took a few minutes to think about it; it is not unique to theism. What is unique to theists in this conversation is that they believe the almighty creator of the universe does not exist in a "community of Him." He is not traveling through time with us, but He exists outside of time. This is amazing, because our friends and family who move through time with us are forced, as we are, to change as the moments, decisions, and fates push us around.

We just believe that God is steady—really, truly steady.

Understanding Theism 101: Theists believe that our mortal bodies are held within the boundaries of a time frame we call "life." We enter into a world at a point on the timeline that includes the lives of millions of others, and for the most part, we begin our journey through days and years with the guidance of parents and siblings and the most recent of our ancestors rooting us on. In the absence of tragedy through disease, accident, or war, most of us enjoy the blessings of growing into adulthood and having children of our own. Almost everybody believes at least some of this to be true.

Theists believe we find meaning by attaching ourselves during our life journeys to an awareness of God's personal plan for our time in the bigger timeline. To a large degree, our worth or value continues after our souls pass out of the time frame that defines our lives. What is left after we have passed on is likely going to be defined in one of two ways: either we leave a legacy to further guide and be enjoyed by others, or we leave behind a burden in the form of a weight that others must pick up and carry.

Theists believe that a life well-lived with planned and implemented concern for others will always result in a blessing. Wouldn't it be wonderful if the worst thing about our death was that we died?

Understanding Theism 101: For biblical theists, there is a moment in time in which Jesus uttered the words *It is finished* (John 19:30). This is a miracle. The God who stepped out of eternity to take His place among us measured His life in the same way that we measure ours—from beginning to end, from start to finish. When Jesus said these words, He was telling us that He did the complete journey. He could have shouted, "Ta-daa!" and jumped from the cross. He could have said, "You fools actually thought I would submit to this?" and thrown a lightning bolt. He could have dragged that crucifixion out for about three months and said, "I told you so."

But He said that "it," His life measured out by time, was finished. And He did what we all do at some point on the timeline—He died. When He showed up again, the laws of nature no longer applied to Him, what with the walking-through-doors (John 20:19, 26) and flying-into-the-sky stuff (Acts 1:9, 10).

Chapter 8

Theism and Humanity

Our sixth defining question regarding the nature of theism is, What is a human being? Theists believe a human being is a purposeful creation of God that somehow contains elements of God's personality. Life only began once. We believe it happened thousands of years ago when God breathed life into man. Then that single life was passed on, life unto life.

Understanding Theism 101: Practicing theists believe several different things about the nature of human beings. We believe, for instance, that God created humankind and gave life to one man. This is our own simplistic application of Occam's razor to the age-old chicken/egg question. I know that when practicing theists apply themselves to the political conversation regarding abortion, we often try to set a time for when life begins: at birth, at viability, when sperm meets egg, and so on. That attempt at advantageous expediency might be useful to save some unborn children, though it does not appear to help. People do what they are going to do. It is, however, less than honest when considering what practicing theists consider the answer to the question, When does life begin? For the practicing theist, life began once, when God breathed into the inanimate nostrils of the first man His breath of life, and it is passed on, life unto life—Eve from Adam's body, then through childbearing.

It may help explain a bit why we are so danged charged up about abortion, even when it is somebody else's body and concern. Practicing theists believe that to abort that continued life from antiquity that has found its way into a new individual is a violation of the sacred. We often fail to recognize that those from other worldviews do not attach the meaning that it is sacred to human life. This does not solve the argument. It just explains one facet of the discussion.

By the way, theists do not generally believe that "monkeys" is a good answer to chicken/egg research. We still have the same problem of what came first.

Understanding Theism 101: Practicing theists believe that the clump of cells often referred to as a fetus is an actual person, from conception forward. Since we also believe that all persons are endowed with certain rights, we believe that those rights must be extended to all persons without exception, including unborn persons. This inherently means that no one person's rights may infringe upon another person's rights. In essence, I do not hold the right to claim your property, time, or life as my own. This is why theists are often unsympathetic to the argument that "it is my body."

Theists should be empathetic to other worldviews, no matter how strongly we disagree or how serious the consequences may be. I think that empathy to other positions may be the only real first step toward changing somebody's mind.

Understanding Theism 101: Practicing theists do not answer many questions the way one would expect. For instance, Are people basically good? is a question that many of us want to answer with a quick yes. However, in all three basic theistic expressions, there is an underlying assumption that everyone is off track with God—even folks like Gandhi and my grandmother. Practicing theists believe we have a critical need to be made right with God.

Understanding Theism 101: Practicing biblical theists are very much into an idea known as redemption. We believe we were created good, speaking of the moral condition, but we went seriously off track. We believe everyone has. We are acceptable only when we are redeemed by Christ. We like redeeming everything. We put the lyrics of "Amazing Grace" to any song in four/four time, such as the *Gilligan's Island* theme song, "Peaceful, Easy Feeling," or about anything, just to redeem those tunes. Heck, the original "Amazing Grace" tune that we sing in church was a redeemed bar song about loose women! This might explain why we like Christmas so much. We know that many ideas about Christmas are less than pure. Redeem them!

Understanding Theism 101: All three major religions of monotheists believe that our mortal bodies are occupied by immortal souls. We believe that our souls retain our personal identities after death, but without the constraints of time. Christian theists in particular believe the model of life-after-death is revealed by the example of the bodily resurrection of Christ. We will have physical bodies, as opposed to the Hollywood cartoon vision of wings, harps, and clouds. People who orient their perspectives from other worldviews might struggle with the theist's pie-in-the-sky hope of reuniting one day with friends and family, but theists think there is reason to hope. It is why we say things like, "I can't believe he is gone." He. Gone. Something internal tells us death is not the end. It would surely appear as wishful, idiotic thinking to some, but to theists, it is their hope. It is also their greatest fear because of that dang judgment piece. For me, I will someday swing on the rope of the promise of Christ into eternity. I hope.

Understanding Theism 101: Practicing theists have an easier time discussing consciousness within the context of their worldview than do atheists. For a theist, "you" are an individual distinct from your physical body and contain intellect, will and soul. You continue to exist absent from your body upon the death of that body. For atheists, what "you" are is heavily debated. The consensus is that you are conscious by virtue of neuron-based activity in your brain that is capable of retrieving memories and that is extinguished upon the death of the physical body. The big debate among atheist philosophers in the area of consciousness regards free will and morality. This should sound familiar to biblical theists. The idea is you are always reacting naturally, which would mean you are never really choosing a behavior. Every response is automated by nature, a reaction to a stimulus that causes other reactions that cause more reactions. It is interesting reading.

Understanding Theism 101: One of the primary presuppositions that practicing theists hold is that they believe we were created by an intentional desire of a thinking God. All three big religions included in theism teach this to be true. There are consequences to this belief, both good and bad.

One of the consequences was framed for me within a conversation I recently had about "victimless" crime or behavior. He was arguing that porn and consensual sexual activity were generally victimless if he was hurting nobody. There is an obvious point on which we agreed: some pornography takes advantage of weaker individuals. He agreed that would be wrong, of course, but he was arguing for his right to enjoy life on his own terms and the terms of consenting others. "It is my choice," he emphasized repeatedly. In fairness to him, and due to the two-paragraph rule I generally impose, his arguments were more complex and quite nicely fulfilled the tenets of his own worldview of existential humanism. The problem is that we could never agree with each other unless one of us changed our perspective. Theists believe we are not our own. We are owned, almost like slaves in many respects, by God. Biblical theists take it a step further. We were made by God, rejected Him, and then were purchased back to Him, saving us from hell, by the death and resurrection of the Son of God. So we think we sin even when we are the only victim. And that is why we do not have as much fun as we could.

Understanding Theism 101: Christians believe they and all other buttheads in the world are created by a loving God. *Everyone*, including the Dutch as I reference Austin Powers (Myers 1997), is an intentional work of an interested Creator. Therefore, all practicing Christians look for the fingerprint of the Creator in everyone they encounter. Nonpracticing Christians do not look for God in anyone who makes it tough. Be like Jesus and find commonality in odd and unusual places.

> "But Jesus, when did we see You on the street corner begging and gave you a dollar, and when did we see You take a subsidized cab ride to the Emergency Room when all you had was a cold and offered you a Kleenex anyway? When did we see You fighting for BLM and ask You why You were so angry, and when did we sit next to You in Taco Bell when You showed up in a hijab? When did we give

You a high-five when the Raiders scored a late touchdown against our beloved Broncos, and when did we enjoy a hot dog with You at the company picnic even though You were the wealthy boss?"

And Jesus replied, "I tell you the truth, when you did this for all those dorks, you did it for Me" (Matthew 25).

Understanding Theism 101: While discussing the concept of humanity with a naturalist friend, I remarked that his personal respect for others offered significantly more dignity for humanity than his scientific beliefs would seem to dictate. He said that he felt any human being deserves as much dignity and respect as he can give simply because we live in a harsh and cruel world, and every person should be celebrated as a survivor. I enjoyed his defense for human dignity.

Theism has core principles that speak for the dignity of all humans. Christians believe that each person has within them the capacity to be a dwelling place for God. Muslims are directed to honor all descendants of Adam. Jewish theists are told that God created all humanity in His own image. Our problem is that we theists often forget to respect those who do not agree with or follow our religious beliefs.

A respect for the dignity of others should continue in the face of even major differences. Jesus said in the Sermon on the Mount that when we like only those who are similar to us, we are not that impressive (Matthew 5:47). Anybody can do that. We are even to love our enemies. Some theists feel like they are betraying their faith by embracing friendships with those from other faiths or no faith. For sure, we need to reserve our closest relationships for those with whom we can relate on the most important issues. I am pretty sure I can have lunch with a gay dude and not become gay myself. He did convince me to have the salmon, and it was actually pretty good. Offering dignity can be rewarding.

Understanding Theism 101: Let us do a post regarding the nature of humankind in the theistic experience. We believe human beings are created in the image of God. So we are all giant human heads floating among the stars? Not really.

Well, then, what does it mean to be created in the image of God? I'm going to expand upon some ideas from *The Universe Next Door* (Sire 2009).

We possess personality. That means each one of us has a combination of characteristics or qualities that distinguish us from others. It gives us identity. We are self-aware and self-conscious. So is God. In fact, one of the best things about our communion with God is when we focus on those wonderful attributes of His nature. It is just an image. We are not exactly like Him, but we are like Him in that we have identity and personhood. Did you ever notice that *person, personality,* and *personal* are all close to the same idea? This is one way we are created in His image.

We are capable of self-transcendence. We can perform significant actions that are outside of our immediate selves. We can not only throw a ball and break something, but we can move others through our words and actions. We can create things. We cannot create exactly like God, because He created everything from nothing. This is called creation ex nihilo. But we can create music and paintings and software programs. This part of what we understand God to be is a beautiful and wondrous part of our humanity.

We possess intelligence. Well, most of us do. Okay, the women do. Intelligence is a key part of the nature of God, and to be made in His image means that all of us, even the guys, possess different measures of knowledge and the ability to discern and decipher the world around us. In biblical theism, we are warned that God's intelligence is above our own and that we cannot possibly know His mind, but the gift of thinking He has provided us with is used at its best to understand and develop a mind for God as best as we possibly can.

We possess a moral code. Somewhere within us lies a moral compass that bears the image of the creator God. He is perfectly right and never wrong. We have to just trust this. The thing that is so wonderful to me about this moral compass is that it operates just like a normal compass. True north is outside of the compass, pulling the needle into alignment. True right is outside of us, but we have an inbuilt sense for right and wrong. C. S. Lewis begins his masterful defense for the existence of God by discussing this innate awareness of right and wrong in *Mere Christianity* (C. S. Lewis, Mere Christianity 1952, renewed 1980).

Sire uses the term *gregariousness* to discuss another aspect of the idea that we are created in God's image (The Universe Next Door: A Basic Worldview Catalog, Fifth Edition 2009). This simply means that humans are social and community-oriented. We are fond of company. In biblical theism, we have a difficult but important theology that says God is three in one: the Father, the Son, and the Holy Spirit. Community is built right into this image. We rarely seek to be loners; even when we are harmed by family or community, we still desire to be connected.

Understanding Theism 101: Theists are taught from their texts that we must recognize that all people are endowed with reason. This is not to say some do not have a very broken ability to reason, but the exception is not going to break the rule. We also believe people are created with free will and enjoy the privilege that comes with bearing the responsibility for their own decisions. In short, we believe that people can think, and that they have freedom to express their thoughts or feelings in a multitude of ways.

Theists believe that reason and free will leave us with an obligation to seek truth. We know that if we were prevented from the ability to act upon our own reason and free will by another person, religion, or government, we would know we were being unfairly oppressed. Turnabout is fair play, and we should offer the same freedom to any other person, even if our own kid has a different worldview.

Understanding Theism 101: Theists all have a version of what we know as the Golden Rule. I really love how it is expressed in Islam: "None of you believes until he wishes for his brother what he wishes for himself" (Hadith #13). Judaism tells us, "That which is hateful to you, do not do to your fellow. That is the whole Torah; the rest is commentary" (b.Shabbat 31a).

Christianity, of course, tells us through Jesus, "Do unto others as you would want them to do unto you" (Matthew 7:12).

All of this is among the most complete of the summaries of our faiths that we know. All the summaries urge us to behave toward others the way we would like to be treated. It is so simple, or it should be, but in practice it can be tough. Theists are obligated to think through their reactions and to act according to these principles.

A side note: I recently got a fortune cookie that told me to "do onto others as I would do onto me." I spent the day putting hats on people.

Understanding Theism 101: I tried to defend the theistic principle of respect for life to a friend once. She laughed at me that I would say Muslims and Christians respect life. Her statement against Muslims was regarding the fringe who kill people in the name of Allah. That was hard to defend because our discussion started with thoughts on the Boston Marathon bombing. Her argument against Christians involved three issues: (1) pro-war and pro-gun politics, (2) the death penalty, and, believe it or not, (3) being anti-abortion, which in her mind meant we do not care for the lives of the affected mothers or for the babies who are not aborted, but who grow up in horrible circumstances. The fact that I could not convince her that most theists value life very highly was too bad.

We need to balance our love for life with love for people who are alive. We might show better.

Chapter 9

Theism and Afterlife

The seventh question in our quest to define theism is, What happens to us when we die? We continue to exist, and after death we will face judgment. That judgment will be by God, and the result is an eternal reward, which we know as heaven, or an eternal punishment in the form of separation from God, which we call hell.

Understanding Theism 101: Practicing theists believe we will continue to exist as individuals even after we die. We believe our life choices have eternal consequences. This might help explain why we are often party poopers.

Understanding Theism 101: Practicing theists believe that when we die, we continue to exist. We believe that after we die, we will be judged by God for the choices we have made on this earth. One of the unique positions of biblical theists is that they are aware their behavior can never be good enough to pass any judgment by a perfect God. Thus, the only choice of any real consequence that we make during our lives is the choice to accept what the Bible calls the free gift of Christ. It is difficult to explain, and we know we do not deserve it, but that is what we mean when we say we are saved. Therefore, we often make decisions that seem very shortsighted, like staying in marriages that others might leave. We will suffer doing the right thing on earth so we do not get into eternal trouble. As practicing theists, we do not think we are better than others; we just think we are saved from our badness, and we think you should be, too. That is why we act holier than thou.

Understanding Theism 101: What happens to you when you die? Practicing theists believe two things very strongly. First, it is not the end for us. We believe we will continue to exist in some form or another. Second, we believe that our creator God will confront us after we die, and that we will face some sort of accounting for our time on earth. Biblical theists are positive that without the intervention of Christ, we will come up short in that accounting. Therefore, we often feel compelled to share Jesus. We cannot keep our religion to ourselves. We love people and we believe that everyone we know will be held accountable for our decisions. We have to say so.

Understanding Theism 101: Practicing theists of all types believe that our time on earth is just a flash when compared to our real life. This stands in contrast to the atheistic worldviews, which basically see experiential existence as being confined to the cradle-to-the-grave scenario. Just think for a moment how those two perspectives play out in life. Practicing theists will often choose to suffer through a terrible situation just because they feel "this is only earth." The practicing atheist will understand that since we live only once, it is better to cut bait and move on to a different pond. Sometimes this makes us nervous when we see YOLO, the idea that "you only live once." We don't believe the sentiment. We do YLF: "you live forever."

Understanding Christianity 101: Practicing Christians believe there will be a time when the world and everyone in it will be made right by God. We talk about things like the kingdom coming and lordship to a King nobody can see. Some of us, in our zeal to make the world ready for this coming King, want to scrub the place of every speck of dirt, and we think sin is the worst dirt. We identify sin and sinners, and we stomp, scream, and preach it clean so that when the King returns, the palace will be in order. So hopefully, there will be no smoking or smokers, no drinking or drinkers, no cussing or cussers, no Islam or Muslims, no gay marriage or gays, no overeating or fat preachers, no complaining or complainers. Do you see the problem? The coming King will make things right, but not in the way some professing followers of the King understand.

Practicing Christians need to know this. The coming King has called us to live according to His rule *right now*. The kingdom of God is present when a follower of Christ radically reorients his or her behavior to the rule of Christ. What is the rule of Christ? Is it to hate sin? Only in the sense that sin harms us by separating us and others from God. The rule of Christ is better summed up in the way it was explained to the rulers of the Jewish law. Jesus said that He wants us to love God and to love people.

I teach this stuff every Sunday. If you can find a place where Christianity is taught in this basic way, you not only win at Theism 101, but you also win at life.

Understanding Theism 101: In all theistic religions, death is either a gateway to a new life with God or a gateway to eternal separation from God. The reason we talk about hell is because eternal separation from God is also an eternal separation from every possible connection to the things for which we most aspire. My favorite writer, C. S. Lewis, expressed an idea that hell is the greatest monument to human freedom (The Great Divorce 1945). The plain fact is that God respects you and your favorite people and your greatest enemies enough to allow every person to choose against Him. Does He destroy those who rebel against Him? No. He allows them what they want—a reality without any part of the divine, loving, purpose-filled mind of God. That is why we call it hell.

Understanding Theism 101: Anxiety over death is something that is a concern to about everybody on earth, no matter what worldview they find themselves following. For people who think beyond the moment, this is one of the foremost worldview questions. Theists are often accused by atheists and humanists of choosing theism as a resting point because of its supposedly feathery views on death and what comes after. For biblical theists, the thought of an afterlife is great until we remember we are also subject to a judgment that few of us feel we will pass. That can certainly up the anxiety level, even in the face of the loving nature of God or cartoon heaven.

Psychologist Nathan Hefleck has examined this question, and he concludes that almost every worldview offers comfort from the anxiety of death if that worldview is believed strongly enough (Heflick 2018). The idea is that knowing helps, no matter what you know. So face up to those dragons.

For theists, death anxiety may be abated in one of two ways. The first is never to think seriously about death but keep a generalized hope that it will all be okay because God is love. I do not recommend this approach. I remember counseling with a young lady who lost her faith in God because her ninety-eight-year-old grandmother passed away even though the young lady prayed fervently for her recovery. She did not have room in her view of reality to include the fact that everyone dies. She was surprised by it. If you are worried that she is going to read this and be offended, do not worry. I guarantee she will not read this. Anyone who reads this book will at least have an awareness that everybody dies.

The other way to combat death anxiety from a theistic perspective is to face the question head-on. The sacred writings of all theistic expressions speak profusely about the topic. Not only does the center of biblical theism rest on the promise of Christ that He will conquer death on our behalf, but the empty tomb guarantees that promise. It is the rope of hope on which we all swing out into eternity.

Understanding Theism 101: Biblical theists do not believe in cartoon heaven. We do not believe we turn into angels or devils. We do not believe hell is in the center of the earth or heaven is in the clouds. We do not believe Clarence got a new set of wings when he died, but you get two points for knowing that reference (Capra 1946).

General biblical theology holds that after death we will be judged by Christ, and those who have accepted Him as Lord will be renewed, along with the heavens and the earth. All that is bad, broken, or messed up will be removed, and we will see God for who He is. Jesus said in the book of Matthew that He would also judge those who have chosen against Him to be forever separated from God.

Eternal choirs are probably not the right vision of what heaven will look like. My biggest question has always remained the same: will there be basketball, and will anyone ever miss a shot?

Understanding Theism 101: Practicing theists obviously believe that after death we continue to live either in fellowship with God and His followers or in separation from God and His creation. There is a theology that is growing more popular among biblical theists that suggests those who do not choose to follow Christ will not be a part of eternity, but that is for another class.

Other worldviews, almost entirely across the spectrum, view death as the end. No wonder theists stand out like a sore thumb. Naturalists, nihilists, humanists, and most postmodernists believe death is equal to oblivion or extinction. Pantheists and polytheists believe death is the end of self, but not necessarily the end of us.

Theists are accused of being afraid of death. I think we are more afraid of the idea of being judged.

Understanding Theism 101: All theistic worldviews include the idea that there is an afterlife. They all include the idea that a single God with personality has serious expectations about what is required of us to engage with that afterlife without being judged as unready to enter the eternal experience with God. In each religious expression of this worldview, God has expectations to which we are not living up. In biblical theism, we are required to encounter ourselves and to recognize that we are not okay with God. We are expected to confess this failure and to make a vow to orient ourselves in a new way, to put ourselves under the trust and direction of Jesus. This requires two basic confessions. The first is that Jesus is the only way we can be made right with God, and we must confess that we cannot do this on our own effort. The second confession is that even though we know we cannot be made right with God in our own strength, we are still going to commit to change our behavior. This is called repentance. We are not required to be perfectly repentant, because that is impossible. But when we fail, we are expected to acknowledge that failure and to try to improve.

Judaism and Islam each have the expectation of repentance in their religious understandings as well. They are more focused on their abilities to sacrifice and obey, without the benefit of the perfect penitent that we have in Christ.

Chapter 10

Theism and Morality

Here is another question to help us define our theistic worldview: How do we know right from wrong? It comes partially from observing natural law but mostly from revealed law through the Bible, Qur'an, or Torah. Our moral compass is external, not internal.

Understanding Theism 101: Authentic theists of all three major religions have an irritating built-in pursuit of perfection that seems to occur right in the face of our decidedly imperfect nature. There is not much more irritating than a Muslim cleric telling us we grow closer to God by killing a woman who has left her abusive husband, or a Jewish rabbi belittling a Palestinian child, or a Christian minister protesting at a funeral of a gay man. But all three of these stories are in this week's news (June, 2017). In each case, sacred texts were utilized as a weapon against a person who fell short of some moral or religious standard. The reason these stories and the hundreds like them are newsworthy is because most of the world sees the hypocrisy.

How does authentic biblical theism address this? One of the beginning points is that we are encouraged to closely examine ourselves, to look into a mirror without forgetting what we see (James 1:22-25). Jordan Peterson says, "I don't think that you have any insight whatsoever into your capacity for good until you have some well-developed insight into your capacity for evil" (45 Minutes on a single paragraph of Nietzsche's Beyond Good and Evil 2017). Solzhenitsyn reminds us that the line that divides good and evil cuts through every human heart (The Gulag Archipelago 1918–1956

1974). Our search for perfection is motivated by a desire to be like the perfect model (for Christians, Christ). We do our best work by focusing on our own character and on our neighbors' needs. My best advice is don't make the news for being more perfect than the rest of us. It never reads well.

Understanding Theism 101: Practicing theists do not believe our hearts have any real, good idea of what is best for us. This might explain a bit of where we are coming from on many political issues. Biblically, for instance, we are told the heart is deceptive above all things. Elizabeth Gilbert (Eat, Pray, Love: One Woman's Search for Everything Across Italy, India and Indonesia 2006) is sort of the counterpoint to theistic thinking on the wisdom of the heart.

Understanding Theism 101: Yesterday's post about theism and morality evoked an incredible discussion that went sideways when a well-meaning friend decided to answer some questions on my behalf. He kindly explained that Christians are the only people in the world who possess the ability to make morally correct decisions because they are the only ones who have the Word of God to guide them.

That is not what theists believe! I apologized before we shut the conversation down, but in the end, I felt like a moron "oxymoroned" his way through a china shop. I will try to explain more clearly.

Even if my friend were on the right track, protecting the absolute value of Scripture or the ability of Christians to interpret God's Word correctly in all instances, or even assuming that theists and atheists had absolutely nothing in common, my misguided (and blocked) friend forgot lots of theistic principles. Let us look at a couple of reasons why theists should believe atheists can absolutely make sound moral decisions. Remember, though, these are not the same reasons atheists might use to defend their ability to be ethically or morally correct.

The first reason a theist should trust that nonreligious friends can be champions of morality is that we believe God created every single person, and His divine touch is present in every single person whether they advocate for Him, follow Him, or deny Him completely. An atheist might not think anything in his conscience is dictated by God, but *we* think it is. Again, these are not reasons atheists think they are moral; these are reasons theists think atheists can be moral. After last night, I cannot apologize or explain things enough.

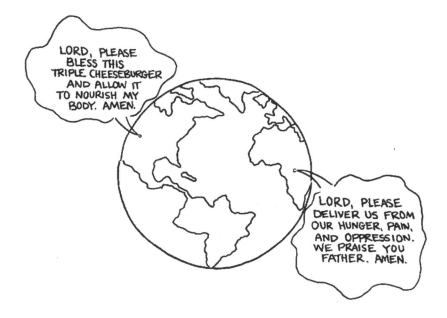

A second reason that theists can trust their nonreligious friends to discern moral truth is because we believe God has chosen more than one way to make His presence and His values known among humans. For sure, we love the specific advice of His revealed ethical constructs through Scripture. But we also learn morality through personal experiences, empirical evidence, and good authorities, including many theistic influences like grandmothers and schoolteachers from years past. I have one atheist friend who is thankful for every meal he takes, and he expresses gratitude because he thinks his mother's old habit helps him to be a better person, even if his thanksgiving is only directed toward the universe and chance.

Understanding Theism 101: Typically, theists judge almost every sexual action outside the confines of marriage as wrong. Theists, in general, are known for two extreme wrongs when dealing with sexual ethics. The first is the error of misogynistic control within or outside of the context of marriage. Islam religiously expresses this control with extreme cruelty. Biblical theists are all over the board, but historically and in the present, they usually look upon such male dominance as cowardly, even though families in our churches are living it out without consequence. That is very unattractive to people who are searching for love and acceptance. The second error is the extreme abdication of masculinity within or outside of marriage.

Practicing biblical theists are directed by their Scriptures to love their husbands or wives, not to lord over them. At the same time, men have special encouragement to protect and to serve their families.

Understanding Theism 101: Practicing theists do not get into the idea that a person "is not that bad." In fact, for biblical theists, we believe the *best* things we do are like disgusting trash. The Bible even refers to it as flushable trash, according to Isaiah (Isaiah 46:12). It is almost like we cannot even give a little money to cancer research without thinking we should have given more or we only gave to look good to others or to God. This seems negative and potentially bad for our self-esteem. Folks from other perspectives might even worry that we are neurotic!

Our problem is not one of comparing ourselves to other people in the world. It is the fact that our behavior and motives must be compared to

110

those of the perfect creator of the world. For a practicing theist, we feel we are lying when we say things like, "I am really a good guy, down deep. I just have a little problem with my temper when I drink." We are not good down deep. Our behavior betrays the truth about us. It gets even tougher when we start to clean up our act. Everybody can hardly wait for Tim Tebow to cuss, drink, or sex it up so they can finally call him a hypocrite! It is the same problem but on the other end of the scale. For a theist, the scale is not an issue, because none of us are righteous. We can only seek righteousness.

This might help to make sense out of why we are always so worried about sin, sinners, and sinning. It is an awful pain to recognize our failures, but it would be dishonest not to admit that our failures separate us from God. Of the three major theistic expressions, the antidote for our problems in Judaism and Islam is to work for righteousness by not sinning, and seeking absolution of some sort when we do commit sin. In biblical theism, we just give up and let Jesus take care of things.

Understanding Theism 101: Practicing theists from all religions have lots of sexual hang-ups. Have you ever noticed that? From homosexuality to premarital no-touch rules all the way to some of us (not me, but others of us) not attending PG movies for fear of seeing a scantily clad vixen, we pull out the holier-than-thou card with lightning speed. It doesn't seem to stop us from being just as naughty as the people we get so upset with. We seem to get caught at that stuff as often as anybody else. But failure to live up to our proclamations does not stop us from making them. I think there are two reasons why practicing theists have so many sexual rules, whether we keep them well or not. Some of us are quite admirable. Not me. But Tim Tebow seems to be amazing.

First, we have written rules in our faith documents. It is as simple as that. The fact that a person from a different perspective thinks the rules are outdated or irrelevant makes no difference; whatever God says outweighs what you, I, or any committee says.

Second, and more important to me at least, is the idea that all theists believe God created us, and as our Creator, He knows what is best for us.

For instance, before we married, my wife and I restrained from what seemed like a good idea at the time. But do you know one thing we both got from that period of abstinence? Trust. We both *know* the other one will not even sleep with someone they love if it is not right. It has made more than thirty trips overseas without her no problem at that level.

Plus, I'm a fraidy-cat.

Understanding Theism 101: I heard a new term the other day to describe under-thirty unmarried Christians who are sexually active. The term is *sexual atheists* (Luck 2014). Well, that is cute, but it is a worldview inconsistency. Theists do not get to pick the practices they want to follow and just ignore the rest. The author rightly suggests that such a philosophy results from a combination of a low regard for scripture, and a high regard for self. That is called deism. Deists cannot be practicing biblical theists. It does not work that way. We do not get to retain the right to call ourselves Christians when we abdicate scriptural norms.

Understanding Theism 101: Theists tend to be pro-industriousness. That means theists believe that begging, mooching, and laziness are bad for your soul. That does not mean theists hate the idea of caring for those who are in need. Our sacred texts speak highly of concern for our neighbors, especially those who are in poverty or pain. Judaism is replete with the idea that God literally has the back of the one who looks after the poor. My Muslim friend who runs the Islamic prayer house in my hometown is obligated to welcome the traveler, no matter who or why, and to put them up for the night if they are approached. Jesus tells us to give until it hurts. This is a paradox, for sure, but it is one way theists must stay diligent in working out their faith.

Understanding Theism 101: There is a new thing out there and it is driving me crazy. I know why it bugs me; I just do not want to admit it. It is called virtue signaling, and it simply means "I am better than you."

Let us face it—this used to be the moral high ground of the biblical theists, where we perched with our pride for moral superiority and peed upon the unwashed and undignified masses below. Now all of a sudden, wacko environmentalists and social justice warriors of every type have flanked us and taken the moral high ground. I think I am jealous!

Remember the good old days when a cake maker could refuse to make a cake for a sinner? Well, now people who love and care for the person the cake maker rejected are telling the cake maker that they are better people than he is because he likes religious cakes more than he likes people! They kind of ruin it when they want the cake maker to die an unemployed death, but let's be honest—we Christians also often fail to hold our moral high ground with dignity.

Understanding Theism 101: Practicing theists often find themselves facing a dilemma where they are forced to choose between what normal people would think is right and what they understand to be right according to their sacred (read: old) texts. It is understandable that those who do not believe in a God with a personality would have no use for any document that considers any behavior to be sinful, as any such document must arise from imaginary pretenses. For theists, however, it is the belief in the supernatural universal prime cause that takes precedence in their battle to do right. We might want to say, "I now know better, and the old law is outdated." What would come next is more than a theist could stomach: "And if the old law is outdated, therefore, God is gone or never was." We just do not believe that, so we hold to old rules. Jesus made it easy for biblical theists when He said to love God and love your neighbor.

Understanding Theism 101: Practicing theists believe the basis for ethics and morality is contained within the character and nature of God and is reflected through mankind. Each of the major theistic expressions also believes that certain disconnects with God's moral nature, such as sin or ignorance, may cause us to fail at perfectly living up to the moral code. So, on one hand, we think God provides insight to guide our ethical behavior, and on the other hand, we find ourselves unable to live up to the expectations of God (C. S. Lewis, Mere Christianity 1952, renewed 1980).

In each of the theistic expressions, "getting right" with God is important. For many theists, getting right is attempted through good deeds. Biblical theists believe that good deeds always fall short and count on being "justified"—not through behavior, but through the help of Jesus, who acts as a substitute on our behalf. That is why we like Him so much. It also speaks to the fact that biblical theists understand why others see hypocrisy in our ranks. We do not really think we are better than others. For the record, the best person I have ever known was an atheist named Dave. We just think we are forgiven, and not because we deserve it, but because we accept the offer of forgiveness.

Understanding Theism 101: Practicing theists are often accused, and rightly so, of being less than fun. Some practicing theists couldn't let their hair down if they wanted to because it is always cut too short (above the ears kept my grandma happy). In the theistic worldview, fun is not a high value. Neither is personal happiness. They are valued, just not highly. Both concepts are heavily moderated by responsibility and integrity...way heavily moderated. It has to do with what might be called end-game thinking. For many worldviews, end-game thinking encompasses two main ideas: death and concern for others. The extreme can be called YOLO: *you only live once*, so get as much living in as you can. Concern for others moderates dangerous and illegal behavior, but even then, a humanist, for instance, might encourage a friend to sow some oats so as not to waste precious life.

End-game thinking for theists goes past death, and life is just a flash in the pan to a theist. Dustin Hoffman and Warren Beatty sang it well in *Ishtar* (May 1987): "Life is just an audition for God, let us pray we all get the job." Anyway, practicing theists really limit themselves, hoping for a payoff in the end. This is end-game thinking. I tend to encourage my kids this way: Seek happiness, and you will never really find it. Seek character, and happiness will catch you from behind. I am fifty-nine years old and feel that sentiment has been proven in my life. I have totally missed some easy fun along the way, but I am happy.

Understanding Theism 101: Practicing theists believe God has established the principles of right and wrong regarding morals, though they often disagree greatly as to what those principles mean in action. C. S. Lewis (Mere Christianity 1952, renewed 1980) said this moral code is not relative, but it is "as hard as nails." Practicing theists believe each individual is responsible for understanding and responding to this moral code. Therefore, theistic responses in assigning responsibility to yesterday's tragedy at the school in Connecticut tend to go in two directions: the individual who committed the act and the individuals who can help restrain their neighbors in future attacks. They do not look to society, culture, or government to help. I think this is one reason we divide from other worldviews on the gun control issue. It is almost always the theist who puts the "guns don't kill people, people kill people" bumper sticker on their car, right?

Understanding Theism 101: Practicing theists believe in loving their neighbors. C. S. Lewis once said that to love our neighbors, we sometimes must restrain other neighbors to the ultimate degree (God in the Dock: Essays on Theology and Ethics 1970). How vacant of moral aptitude does a person have to be to take a gun to a kindergarten class to make a point? There are bad people in this world; some are little Hitlers. Practicing theists believe evil is real and palpable. What happened to the children of Sandy Hook in Connecticut today (December 14, 2012) is not simply poor fortune—it is real, unadulterated evil. No matter how hard it is to explain God in the face of such atrocities, it is just as hard to deny that evil is real when our gut instinct tells us clearly that evil has come into our lives.

Understanding Theism 101: Practicing theists believe moral truth is revealed through God's written words. We think the God who created us is personal, and that God communicates with us in ways that we understand, though it is somewhat murky. We believe He communicates with us through sacred writings such as the Torah, Qur'an, or Bible. He also teaches us truths through nature, where His power and awesomeness are revealed in obvious ways. This is why we sometimes seem to lack common sense. We are often told through these writings to do the thing that betrays common sense. Some of these things appear to be hateful, like standing against certain monogamist expressions of marriage. Sometimes these writings are amazing, such as telling us to love our enemies. We deeply believe not only that God's ways are not the same as our ways, but that His ways are above our ways.

Understanding Theism 101: Theists stubbornly do one of two things regarding the gender debates. The first is to root themselves unbendingly to the oldest of fashions when it comes to accepting anything other than male and female. We do not even like unisex T-shirts. Many outside of theism cannot even fathom how we can be so shortsighted. The other extreme is to embrace all gender questions with two principles in mind: Jesus loves everybody, and who am I to judge another's reality or feelings?

The problem with the latter approach is that it is difficult to square with authentic biblical theistic reality. Yes, Jesus loves everybody, and so should we. That does not mean He does not ask us to change behavior or not to surrender ourselves to His rules of order. In theism we can be authentically wrong. The Bible has little to say about gender, but it has a lot to say about the two sexes, male and female, and the proper plan for how we relate to each other. Trying to explain it away as misunderstood Scripture or poor interpretation is as silly as trying to tell me why two plus two does not equal four. It really is just there, and the only reality that matters is God's.

That does not give the first group of theists from the opening paragraph free rein to march, protest, and separate themselves from the LGBTQ+ world. We must love them and call them neighbors in the best of all ways. We can be near people without fear that they will make us believe what they believe, and we must be near people without giving approval to things we would call sin. My wife says something interesting: "Your sexual orientation is the eighty-seventh most interesting thing about you to me." I love that, but it is a difficult thing to hear by someone whose sexual identity is the most important understanding they have of themselves. That gives me a lot to think about.

Understanding Theism 101: No matter what worldview you might have, you are a moral person. Your decisions and actions are either good or bad. Your morality is defined by your worldview. How you answer specific questions about the meaning of nature, history, social meanings, and constructs; what happens when you die; and so forth is going to define your morality. Theists have a lot of interest in moral right and wrong. In fact, our uptight sense of moral outrage is the most endearing thing about us, right?

Maybe not.

Well, perhaps I can explain just a bit about practicing theists and morality. For theists, moral absolutes are supernaturally revealed. This is unique to theism. If you are not a theist, this seems stupid, moronic, and careless. Those of us who are theists really believe in the supernatural, so it does not seem as far-fetched to us. In fact, some of the best treatises written on the existence of God were written by brilliant and highly educated people such as Thomas Aquinas, C. S. Lewis, and N. T. Wright. They freely use immeasurable ideas such as fairness, beauty, justice, and love to prove the deity thing. One of the most important aspects of supernaturally revealed moral codes is that they are timeless. We hold to some old ideas, no matter what the new advances are. Most other worldviews perceive of moral right and wrong in relative terms—relative to culture, time, and whatever is politically correct or even politically right.

Fortunately for biblical theists, our code boils down to loving God and loving people. Even that is exceedingly difficult. Our moral outrage often stems from the fact that we are standing on moral shores while the rest of the world is floating in the river of relativity. While theists scream at the world, "You are wrong!" the world screams back, "Who are you to judge?" Are we ever going to get along? I doubt it, but if you sinners would just let me complain, it would go a long way toward world peace!

Understanding Theism 101: If you consider yourself to be a spiritual person yet find yourself completely frustrated by your theistic friends, whether they be Muslim, Jewish, or Christian, one of the issues that needs to be understood surrounds the question of tolerance. Worldviews other than theism that include the supernatural (polytheistic or pantheistic, naturalistic humanism, deism) all include a willingness to raise levels of tolerance. This is true for almost anything other than naturalistic atheism. Usually, this is equated with an open mind and is seen as a valuable character trait. It can even be seen as loving.

Theism requires lower levels of tolerance because the parameters for truth are focused in the writings of our sacred texts. For instance, practicing theists do not have the option to be open-minded about sexual ethics without abandoning the texts that define their faith. Do not make the silly statement that we should just give up archaic values. We can no more do that than you can toss your grandmother to the curb for still using trans fats in her chocolate chip cookies. We believe God made the world and He wrote a book about it. Consider this: in mechanical engineering, the most expensive products are engineered to the lowest degrees of tolerance. Fine- tuning and demanding specifications make things work better.

I would also say this about tolerance in general: judgment is better than tolerance— *always*—as long as it is right judgment or judgment with all the facts. I always say that nobody in their right mind would let Hitler babysit their children. He is dead and would be a terrible babysitter. Our worst problem with judgment is when we judge prior to fact gathering. Prejudging. Prejudice. See that? I am not a tolerant person, but I have given money to a Muslim friend to start a barber shop in a Nairobi slum. I have posted photos online because I was proud of his effort.

For nontheists who do not get why we will not bend, I hope this helps. Sorry, though. I have nothing to say about the theists who must be total jerks in explaining their point of view. Remember, I can only speak concerning practicing theists. On the same front, I have no sensible answer for the tolerant people who cannot tolerate people who think differently than they do. By the way, I do want to be open-minded, just not so open-minded that my brains leak out (Taylor, Guilty by Association from Meltdown 1984).

Understanding Theism 101: Practicing theists are often accused of being less than sympathetic, even harsh, when coming up against the pain and shortcomings of themselves and others. I was recently asked why Christians, also called biblical theists, sometimes lack empathy for those who are victimized. A big part of the philosophy we espouse is a consideration of the following: empathy is not an unencumbered virtue. It always protects at a cost. It is the mother bear's compassion that will get you eaten. I was in a counseling situation recently where my harsh advice drew an admonition: "Don't you care about me?" My response was, "I care more about who you are going to be." Biblical theists believe Jesus loves you just the way you are, but He loves you too much to let you stay that way.

Understanding Theism 101: Theists can be incredibly loving and charitable. It is part of the reason that hospitals have names like St. Mary's or Baptist Memorial or even the Tim Tebow Medical Clinic. Okay, I don't know about that last one, for sure. This spirit of charity flows from an understanding that a couple of God's primary core values are love and justice. Service and charity to all seem to flow more freely from the biblically theistic framework, especially Catholicism. This is obviously due to the influence of the person-God, Jesus Christ. It also has great moments in theism's other two main expressions, Judaism and Islam.

The other side of this coin, unfortunately, is "terror-fying." Within all three major religious systems that are defined by the theistic worldview are religious adherents who embarrass and mortify their fellows. Often called extremists, these fringe theists have disconnected themselves from God's love for humanity and thrown themselves entirely into a love for one thing only: the destruction of God's ultimate enemy, a humanity that rejects Him. Just as we do not see hospitals called Mercy of Naturalistic Science, we also do not see the Brotherhood of Radical Atheistic Reform claiming responsibility for the fertilizer plant fire in Texas. And, once again, a bomb goes off, and once again, radical Muslims are apparently to blame. Don Marquis has said that "an idea is not responsible for those who believe in it" (Quotes 2021). I do not think God or religion is responsible for people like the nut-job child-killers who were being chased all over Boston last night, but I believe we who have a voice must lead in love.

Jesus spoke to us all when he said, "Father, forgive them, for they do not know what they do." Bono of U2 sings this lyric: "The less you know, the more you believe" ("Last Night on Earth" 2022). That sentiment can go many ways. However, the less we know of God, the more we will think we know what He wants from us.

Understanding Theism 101: Why would an otherwise kind and generous baker refuse to sell a wedding cake to a gay couple? Why would an otherwise devout and religious baker sell a wedding cake to a gay couple? The answer to the first question is that the baker loves the rule of God and desires to honor God through purity and holiness. The answer to the second question is that the baker loves the rule of God and desires to honor God by loving everyone. Does that sound like double-talk? Well, it is not. It is a particularly difficult dilemma. Practicing theists typically struggle with this dilemma of law versus grace, because in all three major religions that share the theistic worldview, God seems to be very interested in both sides of the coin. In Islam we see those who would purify with the sword, but we also see large numbers of Muslims who are so serious about the command to serve the traveler that they leave their mosques open at night for anyone in need. In Judaism we see hardcore followers of Old Testament law, but we also see Jewish people risk their lives to help Palestinian neighbors. We see Christian bakers making cakes and not making cakes. The struggle is real.

Of course, not every decision is made from a devout heart. We may become so proud of our orientation that we judge others for following their own consciences. Some people are just mean, and others do not really care what God desires. I guess if somebody doesn't want to make me a cake, I would look for a different baker.

Understanding Theism 101: Practicing theists believe an external moral guide exists outside of ourselves. In a practical sense, this means we think there are such things as both goodness and evil. They are real things, not just words that describe the kind of luck we are currently experiencing. Pantheists generally understand these experiences as "forces." This is exactly like Star Wars: "Luke, try out the dark side; you will love it over here!"

Atheists do not believe that good and evil exist outside of our social constructs. For atheists, something like murder is wrong because it is socially disadvantageous to the species to behave in such a way, so they apply moral values to certain behaviors. Google it if you do not believe me. The difficult thing in this is that deep down we all seem to *know* that certain things, like pedophilia or genocide, really are *wrong*, no matter what we try to say about truth being relative. This is the most difficult ground for the atheist to stand upon.

Your practicing theist friends get some ideas from this that seem weird to normal people. For one, we agree with the sacred texts that all enforce the idea that the heart is deceitful above all things. We do not follow what seems best to us; we just do what the outside moral influence we call God wrote down for us.

Understanding Theism 101: The ancient Greeks wrote about virtues. Virtues are the seeds from which healthy moral character grows. They spoke of the cardinal virtues, which are the four highest of all the virtues.

The first of the cardinal virtues is discernment. Discernment is the ability to see through the mess and jumble of situations and to really get to the crux of understanding what is going on. Biblical theists believe God wants to assist us in discernment by helping us to no longer conform to the patterns of the world, but to renew our minds according to His direction, which is good, pleasing, and perfect. The lack of discernment as a virtue leads to foolishness. The excess of discernment leads to judgmentalism.

The second of the cardinal virtues is courage. Courage is the ability to do the good and right thing in the face of temptation, pain, or fear. The Bible is full of stories that tell of our heroes of the faith as they overcame threats to their security, acceptance, and significance. The apostle Paul spoke of courage even as he wrote many of his letters from the New Testament Scriptures from prison cells. The deficiency of this virtue is cowardice, while an overabundance of courage could lead to foolhardiness.

The third of the cardinal virtues is temperance. Temperance is the ability to manage or control your own life. It is to be more like a thermostat rather than a thermometer. A temperate person gives control to God and accepts the challenge to be responsible for his own life and decisions. Paul seems to suggest that we must practice this virtue in order to master it. And that is the idea. Temperance is self-mastery. Not respecting the virtue of temperance may lead to licentiousness; while too much temperance, if that is possible, may cause a person to become overly strict.

The fourth of the cardinal virtues is justice. Justice is the desire to see the playing board leveled for all participants. Justice is the ability to wish the same outcome for any other person as you would wish for yourself. It is beyond fairness. Justice is the irritating friend who hangs out with Lady Mercy as she seeks to bathe the world in kindness.

Understanding Theism 101: Anyone notice how many times I referred to C. S. Lewis in this chapter? Perhaps he is worth reading, huh? He notices amazing things about our moral lives and responsibilities.

Chapter 11

Theism and the Nature of Evil

Here's the next question as we further pigeonhole ourselves into a theistic identity: what is evil? Evil is a ruined good. We experience it as a consequence of not following God's plan for us.

Understanding Theism 101: Every self-respecting student of worldviews who comes from a theistic viewpoint must put an understanding of the word *theodicy* into their academic holster. Every post that I present in the Theism 101 series that mentions God and evil can be considered to be a theodicy. A practical definition of theodicy is that it is an attempt to vindicate the passive presence of God in a world where evil not only exists but runs rampant.

If you ever discuss worldviews with someone who is not a theist, and they tell you that you just presented a theodicy, they are probably not complimenting you. To a nontheist, the defense of the notion that God exists, or that a good God exists in the face of evil, is an absurd starting point. They may not even wish to continue a dialogue with someone who believes in theodicies. It might as well be Santa Claus that you are trying to prove.

As a student of worldviews, do not be afraid to offer a theodicy here and there, even in the presence of cynics. Every worldview has its own distinct problem with evil, but rarely is it considered to be as pressing for nontheists. This is because they do not have the existence of God riding on their ability to find meaning within the midst of evil.

By the way, it is pronounced *the* as in theism, and then *odyssey* like what Odysseus did when he got lost. Theodicy.

Understanding Theism 101: The number one reason people reject theism is the fact that evil exists in the world. There is little doubt that if we can handle this most dangerous reality adequately, we can save the reputation of God in the eyes of others, and maybe more importantly, for ourselves. I plan to take a few consecutive stabs at this huge topic in the coming days. I would love for us to build a bit of a foundation from which we might adequately defend our belief system from an attack by a worthy opponent - evil itself.

When theism in general comes under attack by the observation that evil exists in the world, we need to recognize what is happening. The first bombardment is against the existence of God. How can God coexist with evil? Evil attacks our understanding of who God is supposed to be within the context of four very important identities:

(1) God is supposed to be all-powerful. The word theologians use is *omnipotent*. But if God is all-powerful, how can evil be as bad as it is? It would be one thing if evil took a swing at the world, say through a pandemic, and God showed up in a colorful bodysuit with a matching cape and punched that pandemic into outer space, maybe with a Colgate smile and a quick flex before darting off to move an immovable rock somewhere. But that is not what happens. The pandemic hits; and we pray for help from a God who is supposed to be the master of the universe, and the pandemic remains and people die. What the heck?

(2) God is supposed to be all-knowing. The word that the theologians use here is *omniscient*. But if God is all-knowing, why does He allow babies named Adolf to grow up? Surely, He can see into the future and know that certain people are going to cause trouble. Again, we pray to God for wisdom and direction, but we get onto airplanes that are going to crash, and we get married to cool people who turn into devils. What the heck?

(3) God is supposed to be everywhere at all times. The word the theologians use for this is *omnipresent*. But if God is always everywhere, and evil exists, then why doesn't the presence of God overwhelm and destroy evil? How can we pray to God about a cancer within the body of a person we love, ask God to overcome the cancer in a place where He should be able to operate with authority, and then watch our loved one suffer at the hands of an evil that is obviously allowed to exist in the world? What the heck?

(4) God is supposed to be all-loving. The word the theologians use is *omnibenevolent*. But if God is all-loving, why do bad things happen to good people? We pray for God to bless ourselves and others, while we live in a world that knows much more about poverty and pain than it knows about riches and comfort. What the heck?

(WE'RE ALL CONTRIBUTORS)

Anybody with a brain knows that evil is our greatest enemy, not just to our existence, but to our faith and hope. This bombardment against our belief in the reality of an almighty God is just the first attack. Not only am I not going to argue against the ironclad straw man I have presented in this post, but the next post is going to be more bombardment at a different target.

Understanding Theism 101: My previous post discussed the problem of evil for the theist as a real, challenging bombardment against the most basic theme of our faith, our belief that God exists. I was encouraged by the defenses that were raised in the conversation, due to the fact that I left the battle while still under attack. It reminded me of my Methodist childhood and singing "Onward, Christian Soldiers" during every Sunday school class I ever attended. Way to go, and I will use some of your arguments in later posts.

Anyway, let us get bombarded again by a fresh attack from evil itself. If the reality of evil is an attack against the existence of God, it is also an attack against the theist as a person. When our worldview comes under attack, our connection to our tribe is broken. Men have shared about those moments in war when everything they believe is just completely torn to shreds. The violence and senselessness of the moment disconnects them from any sense of planned action, and they retreat into nothing more than a longing for escape from the moment. Once the battle ends, so do their idealism and patriotism. Some recover to find hope in the ideals that allowed them to fight in the first place, while many others limp away from the encounter as cynics. The same thing happens to theists every day, born into homes of faith, thrown into a conflict with pure, nasty evil, and emerging as former theists, wizened by reality. It happens every day in places like middle schools, where children realize they are hated because of ten extra pounds or a preference for anime or simply because they smile too much. It happens because of car wrecks. It happens when a teenage girl with a big heart suddenly realizes that it is her body that is desired by the boys and men she knows.

Evil is real. It exists, and it seeks to destroy. Once again, I am not going to rescue this post from my own observations. I could, and eventually I will, but for now, let us not pretend that evil is not a problem for theists.

Understanding Theism 101: Let us look at one more bombardment by evil against the strongholds of theistic hope. We spoke of the attack against our faith in almighty God. We talked about how evil attacks our faith by ruining lives. Evil also bombards the theist with subtlety. Evil is not only frightfully aggressive, but also as cunningly sweet as honey. This bombardment is from the backpack in the cafeteria. It comes in disguise and hurts all the more because we should have been able to stop it.

What? Evil has a goal. I will discuss the idea that evil has a personality in the future. The goal of evil is to destroy anything that is good. This may happen through blasts of fire and pain, or it may happen through seduction and pleasure. As long as in the end everything good is destroyed, evil wins. Evil dreams of a wasteland. It delights in garbage, the leftovers of a consumed resource. It does not care how the goal is achieved as long as we are used up and tossed aside when it is over.

Evil reaches into the theist's mind and sows seeds of doubt. Why doesn't God care about starving children? Why doesn't God care about me? How stupid can my friends be to keep praying to a God who does not care, who probably doesn't even exist? Then, when doubt has conceived, it gives birth to rejection. When rejection is fully grown, it seeks replacement. And what better way to replace an absent God than by making our own pleasure and experiences the point of our lives? So we indulge the animal desires of our bodies; the things that we pursue, such as money, sex, drugs, and escape. These things will eventually consume us, and evil is glad.

Evil attacks in more ways than these, but theists believe evil is real, and it is the greatest enemy to our faith. If anyone thinks theists are ignorant of the problem of evil, and if they would just pay attention, they could give up their childish faith, well, I want you to know this: we know about evil, and we still believe.

Understanding Theism 101: I think the last several posts about how dangerous the reality of evil is for a theist have been forthright and transparent. The ground upon which we stand is indeed shaken by the reality of evil in the world. Today I am going to fire back at every other worldview adherent.

Your worldview must explain evil as well. In the end, I believe theism provides the most robust defense against evil of all the worldviews. The only other worldview that comes close to having a free pass on the question of evil is nihilism, but nihilists must flip the issue and discuss the good that is rampant in human hearts. Some worldviews deny the existence of evil, saying it is only a word that describes poor fortune, but what about those moments when poor fortune strikes you personally? It is hard to say that the rape and murder of your child was just bad luck. It feels like real evil was inflicted by a malevolent source. Some worldviews hold that evil and good are balanced, as in karma, but there is a heck of a lot more bad happening in the world than there is good. Some Eastern philosophies deny the reality of evil and suffering, so they sleep on beds of nails to prove suffering does not exist.

I have had cancer. It exists.

In one way or another, the other worldviews must take ownership of the problem of evil, but it is largely ignored. Here is an experiment for you to try. Google any worldview plus evil (such as atheism + evil) and see what kind of answers you get. It is mostly why atheists say there cannot be a God. None of it explains the atheist's dilemma with the nature of evil. For some reason, they think God is the only one who needs to explain Himself.

Understanding Theism 101: I have dedicated several posts in succession in recent days to the problem that evil presents to theists. Now let's move on to some favorite theodicies, or defenses of God, in a world where evil exists. There are hundreds if not thousands of theodicies to explore. Many of them weaken the notion of God to make Him more palatable regarding evil, such as suggesting that He is constrained by time, or that the free will granted to mankind has tied His hands. I'm not concerned with those ideas. There are better answers that defend an almighty God. Also, many theodicies ignore the question of evil and simply seek to present airtight arguments for the existence of God outright; they deduce that if God is proven to exist, then there must be some explanation for evil that is beyond us to figure out. I love the proofs, but I think God has given us enough to go on that we can tackle the question of evil as well.

Understanding Theism 101: Where did evil come from? Did God create it? If He did, how can He be good and loving? If He didn't, how can He be all-powerful if there is another spiritual force? How do we explain God and evil side by side?

I agree with C. S. Lewis, who argued in *Mere Christianity* (1952, renewed 1980) that God created everything and that everything God created was good. God granted free will, or the power to choose or reject Him, by putting that tree in the garden. He told Adam and Eve they were free to do anything in the world except one thing: they were not to eat the fruit of that one tree. It was the ultimate respect that God could give them, the ability to go their own way. When they did reject Him by taking the fruit, they literally broke everything good: the earth, themselves, and the future. Everything that may now be considered bad is indeed a broken good. Evil is the brokenness of every good thing given by God.

Understanding Theism 101: Practicing theists believe there is great value in suffering. That is why we sit through sermons and pray in uncomfortable positions. Just kidding, sort of.

There are many theists who assume God does not want us to suffer. They are often surprised to discover that theistic foundations require suffering for many good reasons. Biblical theists are usually the worst. We say, "Why is God doing this to me?" Sometimes we make up excuses for God allowing suffering in life the same way I make an excuse for when my kid misses a free throw in a basketball game: "His legs are tired.".…"He must be punishing me." That might be true, but suffering is part of the game for theists. It allows us to learn and grow. Bonhoeffer said that it is a part of the path to freedom. The whole path is discipline, action, suffering, death, and freedom (*The Cost* of Discipleship 1966). Suffering is akin to discipline, and *no discipline seems pleasant at the time, but later will yield a harvest of righteousness and peace for those who have been trained by it* (Hebrews 12:11 NIV). It is true about the gym, not abusing credit cards, studying math, and becoming what we are intended to be. We are warned that when we do suffer, not to get scrunchy-faced (Matthew 6:16).

Understanding Theism 101: You know my goal here is less about teaching anyone anything about theism and more about helping my non-theistic friends to understand their theistic friends and family. So how 'bout all that evil in the world?

Theists of all three major types are taught from the cradle to hate evil. Many of our teachings are similar to one another, and the way they are expressed, from time to time, look the same to the rest of the world. The three basic ideologies regarding evil are these: (1) run from it, (2) destroy it, (3) rise above it. The runners get chased. I know so many people whose lives have been destroyed by addiction, yet their worst condition is often guilt. The destroyers go wacko really fast—first condemning, then killing, then killing the innocent to make a point. This is the very worst that theism has to offer. The rise-above crowd is in two camps: those who think they are holier than thou and those who really are holier than thou. But everyone hates them equally.

My biblically theistic take on this is we know we are to hate evil, but we are not to hate each other. It seems simple, but it is not, largely because American theists are taught by nearly everyone that they are to value others for such a wide variety of reasons that they cannot separate people from their behaviors. My scroll of Facebook this morning has told me to love people because they are fat, not "even though," but "because." And because they are gay, and skinny, and tall, and their skin is some color, and love guns, and hate guns, and are poor, and need dental work, and they are refugees, and they are gay again, and they might be aborted, and they have female reproductive organs, and they are angry because they are offended, and it never ends. All this advice to love everybody, despite and because of what everybody is and does, or is not and does not do, is very confusing. God loosely says, "Love the sinner, hate the sin." But then, for example, somebody says, "I am gay." What does a theist do with someone who personally identifies as one of our sins? See? It is tough.

We often run from it. We remove not only every rainbow from our lives, but over time any relationship with anyone who scares us. Or we destroy it by beheadings, or the current favorite in the Middle East seems to be tying a forty-foot rope around a human being's neck and tossing them from a fifty-foot building. The less bloody way is to get on Facebook and destroy evil with cruel memes.

Or we rise above it. The biblically hypocritical "rise above" crowd will only rise so far, just barely above their non-judgmental Christian friends.

To really rise above, we must never forget that every human is a child of God, and every move we make must communicate love, and we must never trash our sacred Scriptures. We must remain cognizant of the fact that we will be judged by the same measure with which we judge, and that we are burdened by our own sinful behavior. But we often forget our own failures. That is why it is hard for theists to not come off as jerks.

A final note: Yes, homosexuality is condemned as evil in all our sacred writings. There is no really getting around that. To say, "The texts say no such thing," or "Toss the texts to the curb" is just running from the reality. We must figure out how to love LGBTQ+ and not betray our faith at the same time.

Understanding Theism 101: Practicing theists believe there really is such a thing as evil. This makes for difficulties in all expressions of theism, as we must answer the question, If God is all-good and all-powerful, then why do bad things happen to good people? It often takes a book, or at least a chapter, to answer the question adequately, but usually the approach will include a couple of different points.

Theistic belief is that people are not actually good. Our texts say all have sinned. Theistic belief usually allows for bad because of human corruption, which is easier to explain regarding a murderer than it is for a tsunami or cancer. Theistic belief usually considers that God will set things right, though He hasn't yet. This sounds lazy or bad on His part, but really, it is about giving us an opportunity to self-correct and to seek redemption through God's provision. Practicing theists who think about these things believe it is much easier to answer their troublesome-evil question than it is for atheists to answer their troublesome-evil question: if life and history are undirected and based on chance, why do we think *some* things really are evil and not just bad luck?

Understanding Theism 101: Theists believe it is a good thing to battle against brokenness or evil or wrong in the world. We believe that moral wrongs in self, others, communities, and governments are to be confronted and corrected. Therefore, theists create groups that advocate for the law to conform to ideals and standards that many nontheists believe to be none of our business. For a nontheist, the adage claims that if it does no harm to another, then it should not be legislated against. This makes no sense to a theist. All harm is against God, for a theist. Have you ever heard the abortion argument summed up this way? "My body, my choice." You know what the theist is going to say: "It's not your body!" They can mean one of two things. They could be talking about the body ownership of the fetus-baby thingy, or they could be saying what they believe to be true about their own body, that it is not their own. They believe that to be true about others as well. God owns everything, including the dirt from which we are constructed.

Understanding Theism 101: When theists think about evil, they divide it into two categories, and the only way to determine which is worse is to be caught in the throes of either one.

One kind of evil is natural evil. This would be things like floods, tornadoes, and famines. Cancer and heart attacks can fit in here as well. This is the evil that is hard to blame anyone for, though lung cancer after a lifetime of smoking might be borderline. Natural evil stinks and feels incredibly unfair. I think I handled my cancer like a good theist when somebody mentioned that it was unfair to me, a preacher, a fairly good person, a father and husband, a Christian, a Bronco fan, etc. I said, "Why not me?" Really. What makes me special? I know atheists who are better humans than I am. Do I think it should have been one of them? I know Raider fans that I would not have wished this upon. Natural evil just happens at the same statistical rate of chance to everyone. You win some, you lose some.

Unnatural evil, on the other hand, is meaner. It is targeted and thought up by human minds or is the result of human carelessness (care-less-ness, know the word). Theists really believe there is a special place in hell for the expert releasers of unnatural evil.

Understanding Theism 101: It has been asked, Do I really think Raider fans are evil?

Of course!

Understanding Theism 101: There is a branch of theism that is known only to the most academic of all students of worldviews and religious studies. It is called open theism, and it tries to account for the existence of evil in the world in the presence of an all-knowing, all-loving, and all-powerful God.

This is one of the rare places where atheistic thought is concerned with going head-to-head with theism. Most of the time, naturalist thinkers are not any more concerned about the question of God than I am about landscape design theory within a particular video game. But occasionally the theists make enough noise that the atheists decide to clap back. In this case, atheism sets a claim against the all-powerful and all-loving God either not caring or not being able to prevent the workings of evil in the world. An entire field of new thinkers, called open theists, use an argument that God is innocent of these charges because He operates within the constraints of time, and He voluntarily puts Himself into a position where He allows a future that He does not know to play itself out. It is way more complicated than this, of course, but if you ever hear about open theism, you can know that it is usually a conversation about God, free will, evil, and time.

Traditional theists usually feel that everything they need to have to argue against the uncaring, non-powerful God theory is already available in orthodox theism. Theists are not generally impressed with the idea of open theism.

Understanding Theism 101: Theists believe that evil is intentional and directed against humanity and the world by a fallen angel called Satan (Shaitan in Islam). Not as powerful as God by any means, he dedicates himself to our destruction.

Chapter 12

Theism and Our Ability to Know

O h, look! Here's another question to help us understand the basics of theism: how do we know anything at all? Theists believe God created nature and time to provide an environment for us to connect with Him. We also believe in revealed truth contained in sacred writings that God made accessible to man.

Understanding Theism 101: Practicing theists are typically much more rational than we are given credit. Theism can use all five basic methods of learning to support its foundational principles, just like most other worldview proponents. Theists can, and do, co-opt insights from the worlds of science and philosophy to offer validation for the basic tenets of theism.

My personal favorite reason for being a biblical theist includes a discussion popularized by Thomas Aquinas (The Summa Theologica of Saint Thomas Aquinas, English Translation 1948) called the argument from efficient cause and a similar small syllogism called the cosmological argument. The basic idea behind both is that anything that exists began to exist. The universe exists; therefore, the universe began to exist. Aquinas basically adds that if the universe began to exist, it was caused to exist by an uncaused entity—voila, God! I just summarized huge textbooks into a paragraph, but that is the idea.

Understanding Theism 101: Practicing theists value all methods for obtaining knowledge. The five basic methods that I taught my college students, from weakest to strongest, are as follows: (1) personal experience, (2) empirical evidence, (3) authority, (4) reason/logic, and (5) the scientific method. Even though personal experience is the weakest of the methods mentioned, it is still a valuable process. Simply because the observation is personal is no reason to discount an observation, especially when external confirmations are available. Practicing theists believe that God not only exists, but He has a personality and has an interest in each and every human being. Theists believe, therefore, that God is doing things to make Himself known to individuals. Most of us have made connections in our personal experiences that validate the God-theory for ourselves. On its own, it is not enough, but it does not need to be denied simply on that merit.

This partially explains why theists might pray for help with a parking space while halfway around the world there is a starving child whose requests for food and clean water should be so much more important to God. While my requests to God are embarrassing next to those of an AIDS-infected third-world parent, I still understand that God is interested in me. By the way, practicing theists usually pray for the needs of others much more fervently than they pray for their own needs. Even theists do not admire greed and selfishness.

Understanding Theism 101: Practicing theists believe in absolute truth. The problem is that we often believe we understand absolute truth absolutely. We argue about details. That is why we divide into three major religions—Christianity, Islam, and Judaism—that do not include the salvation of our fellow-worldview adherents. The rest of the world groups us together as the "religious people," yet we have significant faith differences. This observation does not help much, but I just want you to know it is a reality of our situation and a further answer to the question, Why can't we all just get along?

Understanding Theism 101: Freud called it the id, the ego, and the superego—the id being instinctual, personally pleasing, and selfish desires; the superego being your internalized schoolmarm, throwing out warnings and rules; and the ego being that balancing point between getting a lot of what you want but keeping you out of jail. Psych types define the morally mentally ill as those who have little regard for superego influence. It is sort of like the angel on the one shoulder is the superego, the devil on the other is the id, and the real you (ego) is in between. That cartoon illustration is referencing the internal dialogue we face in an ethical crisis.

PERSPECTIVE

Practicing theists have a different foundational belief regarding the superego. We do not believe the superego originates from inside our own heads. Our moral compass is not organically motivated, pointing toward wherever it is we best think is north. We believe north is a real thing apart from ourselves, and that it has a magnetic pull that guides our moral compass to point in one direction. It points toward absolute truth, and absolute moral truth. I have mixed metaphors freely here, but I hope you see my point.

Understanding Theism 101: Biblical theists are often accused of not knowing that the Bible is stupid. I have been told the Bible hates women, supports slavery, and loves murder. And that is just in this week!

There are a couple of things to remember. First, just because the Bible speaks about something, it does not automatically follow that it is in support of the idea. The Bible was written over nearly two thousand years, and believe it or not, Hollywood, music, and sports heroes were not always there to tell us how to behave. The Bible presents stories and lessons within the context of the cultures extant during its writing.

Second, there are plenty of stories, writings, and lessons that should be carefully handled because these stories may be challenging. God does indeed put forth rules and expectations that make no sense in our current context. But that is why we study from the context in which it was written, so that we might extrapolate meaning for our present context.

Understanding Theism 101: Theists and agnostics dance on the same floor. An old Greek word, *gnosis*, means "knowledge." Biblical theists embrace knowledge on one hand but have misused it on the other. In the Scriptures, the book of First John was written to combat the error of gnosticism, which is the idea that as long as you understand something, you don't have to do anything with that knowledge. That is why First John repeatedly says that if you say you have love but do not love your brother, you do not have love. It seems obvious, right? But not so much for a gnostic.

Agnostics (*A* in Greek is "against") are against the idea that we can obtain knowledge through special revelation. It is honest, but in the biblical theist's mind, it is so necessary to getting someone over the bridge. Remember Indiana Jones trying to cross the chasm to find the Grail? The bridge was there, but he did not believe until he saw through the sand what others knew through faith (Ford 1988). This is the dilemma of the agnostic. I hope my agnostic friends are brave enough to toss a little sand now and then.

Understanding Theism 101: A test for worldview validity for every worldview can be called the "test of reason" (Phillips, Brown and Stonestreet 2008). One of the three basic laws of Aristotle's logic is the law of non-contradiction. A worldview cannot have integrity if it is self-contradictory. This is one reason that when I speak of Theism 101 principles, I distinguish between theists and practicing theists. I am suggesting that practicing theists are exercising their worldview in a noncontradictory way. Is this judgmental? Yep.

An example might be some feedback given by a nontheist regarding a Theism 101 statement from last month. I claimed that theists are compelled by the nature of their beliefs to urge others to adopt their worldview because of the following syllogism: we love our neighbors and we believe that we will face a judgment after we die, so we must, therefore, compel our neighbors to come to our viewpoint. It was argued that theists do not have to evangelize.

Many theists believe the same thing, however, practicing theists avoid the law of noncontradiction by recognizing that the basic tenets of their worldview cannot contradict. We believe a relationship with a personal creator-God must be recognized because we believe our existence does not end with physical death. Our love for our neighbors calls us to evangelistic action. Anything less becomes contradictory.

Understanding Theism 101: It is wrongly assumed that science is the weapon of the atheist, and faith in the unseen and unknowable is the only ground for the theist. Here is an interesting little snippet from the foreword of a book I read this afternoon by John Lennox (2011, 12): *"Take for example, the first author on our list, Francis Collins, the director of the National Institute of Health in the USA, and former head of the Human Genome Project. His predecessor as head of that project was Jim Watson, winner (with Francis Crick) of the Nobel Peace Prize for discovering the double helix structure of the DNA. Collins is a Christian, Watson an atheist. They are both* top-level scientists, which shows us that what divides them is not science, but their worldview. There is a real conflict, but it is not science versus religion, it is theism versus atheism, and there are scientists on both sides."

Understanding Theism 101: One of the worldview questions proposed by Sire (The Universe Next Door: A Basic Worldview Catalog, Fifth Edition 2009) is, How do we know anything at all? The theist stands on wide ground here. The answer begins with the belief that truth is absolute and knowable. From there it can be broken into the same five methods I learned in my experimental methodology courses as an undergrad. I think I will cover one per day for the next five days.

Personal experience: It is limited by perspective but absolutely valid. Many theists will share about their experiences with God—how He did this or that, or was there in a time of need, or something that might cause a nontheist to raise an eyebrow of concern. Personal experience is a very weak method for validating any understanding, but just because it is weak does not mean it is invalid. In fact, it is often the first step toward deep validation by other methods. It sort of wakes us up to the question. If you have ever encountered a Mormon missionary who encouraged you to recognize the "burning in your bosom" to validate the truth of their testimony, or if you have ever teared up as Scripture was read at a funeral, you may recognize the appeal to personal experience as a proof of God. Since personal experiences are relative and not objective, those experiences cannot prove the existence of God to anybody else. Again, this does not invalidate the experience; it just must be understood that more is needed.

In coming days, I will mention empirical evidence, authority, reason/logic, and the scientific method.

Understanding Theism 101: Theists believe that truth is absolute and knowable, and that truth can be discerned through all the basic methods of obtaining knowledge that I learned in my experimental methodology class as an undergrad. We have looked at personal experience. It may be weak, but it is valid, and I will now add a second methodology: *empirical evidence.*

Simply put, this is obtaining knowledge by what we observe as we pay attention to what goes on around us. We draw conclusions according to what we see. Things like sunrises, newborn babies, justice, and beauty may cause us to conclude there must be a God. My theistic instruction book, the Bible, even speaks to this. The Old Testament declares that God "placed eternity in the hearts of men" (Ecclesiastes 3:11 NIV). The New Testament mentions that "God's invisible qualities—his eternal power and divine nature—have been clearly seen, being understood from what has been made" (Romans 1:20 NIV). Again, by itself empirical evidence probably does not do the job. When combined with personal experience, it might convince me, but I do not think I could easily convince someone else. But we do not stop here. Tomorrow we will venture into the area of those who read words. Yes, I am talking about smart people! Does this sound judgmental? I never said I was against judgment; in fact, I am for it, but it is quality judgment we must have. Quality judgment gives validity to empirical conclusions.

Understanding Theism 101: For the past few days, I have worked from the idea that theists believe truth and reality are absolute and knowable. Theists use all five of the basic methods for knowing in order to validate their worldview. I have spoken of the two weakest methods, personal experience and empirical evidence, and affirmed the idea that these methods, though weak, are not automatically incorrect. They just need support by other methods. The third method really adds weight to our foundation. It is called the method of *authority*.

Authority may come from many sources, but essentially it is information gleaned from experts. Theists also place authority in their sacred texts. In fact, because we believe our sacred texts are inspired by God, those texts serve as our ultimate authority and often as our ultimate source for knowledge. This very naturally frustrates people from unspiritual worldviews. The important thing to remember is that authority is not the only place theists go for knowledge. Theists should recognize that an existentialist, for instance, does not share the same respect for the authority of the sacred writings. Nontheists, just because you do not value the sacred writings of the theist is no reason to be disrespectful of those writings.

Authority also comes from experts, from great minds. Theists have a boatload of people they are glad to have on their team. My favorite biblical theists include C. S. Lewis, Augustine, Blaise Pascal, and my current favorite, N. T. Wright. Wright has a recent book called *Simple Christianity*, for instance, in which he proves the existence of the Christian God through the concept of justice. It is hugely fun for me (I am a boring person) to watch some of these authorities debate worldview issues. I will watch William Lane Craig all day long. You can YouTube him against your favorite.

I want to mention that we all, not just theists, have authorities that may be less reliable because of the academic rigor applied and more reliable because we like or love those sources. I am talking about places of authority called Mom and Dad, friends and peers, favorite singers, and LeBron James. Just because someone said it does not mean it is legit. Check those sources!

Next, I will look at reason and logic.

Understanding Theism 101: Continuing with the "how theists know anything at all" track, I have mentioned that theists use all five basic methods of understanding and learning. I have talked about the weak but not invalid method of personal experience. I have talked about the added perspective of empirical evidence. I have written a couple of paragraphs on the method of authority. Today I want to mention the method of *reason and logic*.

Reason/logic is highly discounted these days. The main reason that logic is not as useful as it was in the past has to do with our general inability to think and dialogue critically. There are only three real rules to logic: (1) if it is true, it is true; (2) if it is false; it is false, and (3) it can't be both true and false in the same way and at the same time. You would think we could handle three rules, but we can't. There are hundreds of ways to violate the rules. Logic statements are called syllogisms, and since we hated word problems in math class, we have trouble with syllogisms. The famous one is, "Socrates is a man, all men are mortal, therefore Socrates is mortal." So easy, but consider the following: "Umpires have good eyesight, carrots are good for eyesight, therefore all umpires eat carrots." It sounds so close to the first one, but it is not true. It violates the three rules of logic in at least eight different ways; the big one is called an "inconsistent middle term." So, logic is tough.

Personally, when it is done correctly, I believe it far outpaces the fifth and "best" method to obtain knowledge, the scientific method. C. S. Lewis was a master at logic. I really love listening to William Lane Craig debate, but nobody seems to see what he is doing with logic. He is a virtuoso, not lying or manipulating, but masterfully building one idea upon another. Then some guy says, "Duh-h-h, he's too simple. He must be an idiot."

Understanding Theism 101: My last several posts concerning theism have looked at four of the five basic methods of human discovery, and I have suggested that theists like them all. The methods build a solid foundation, allowing us to declare that we can know certain things. In order of generally accepted (by academia more than theists) methods, we go personal experience, empirical evidence, authority, reason/logic, and now, *scientific method*.

Wait! Theists hate science. It is our mortal enemy—not. Theists have many proofs for the existence of God from each of these methods, and for many of us, the scientific method is fearlessly embraced and leads many scientists to conclusions that support the God-hypothesis. Almost 20 percent of graduate-degreed American scientists identify as personally "very theistic" (Ecklund 2010). Scientific issues such as the fine-tuning of the universe for allowable life, irreducible complexity, and the second law of thermodynamics are just a few of the areas that egghead theists love to get on a roll about.

Two more quick thoughts: First, scientific method is the best way to learn anything for sure, but it requires two elements: repeatability and absolute control. Absolute control can never be perfectly attained, thus the thesis/hypothesis/synthesis/thesis world of the scientific journal. Second, the worldview known as agnosticism is basically a worldview that questions our ability to know anything at all. The five methods for taking in information, when combined with philosophical approaches (ontology, epistemology, and ethic), give us fifteen different frameworks from which to consider questions of the universe. How many more do we need to start drawing some conclusions?

Understanding Theism 101: Practicing theists are regularly accused of holding on to a childish worldview. Don't believe me? Take the praise-the-Lord challenge. Post that phrase into any Facebook video of a turtle being rescued from a coyote and wait for the haters: "Fairy tales have nothing to do with the fortunate rescue of turtles!" There is also a lot of "this day and age" and even a fair amount of "what kind of an idiot." As an adult with multiple degrees and a better than average understanding of the correct application of Aristotelian logic, it is always surprising to be told by an eighteen-year-old with a "beleeve in you're self" tattoo that my reasoning skills are lacking. But I do get it. A super childish understanding of my worldview would probably boil down to fairies granting wishes. I even know some devout adherents of the faith who are not much deeper than that type of naivete. However, seriously deep thinkers throughout history have approached questions about good and evil, what's beyond nature, and where stuff comes from without abandoning theism. Some have even been driven toward theism in the end. C. S. Lewis referred to himself as the most dejected and reluctant convert from atheism that the world has ever known (Surprised by Joy 1955). I guess I am just suggesting that all worldviews are worth understanding.

Chapter 13

Theism and the Meaning of Life

The next question to help us to identify the deeper meaning of theism is, What is the meaning and purpose of life? For theists, the purpose of life is to connect with and to be made right by God. It is to recognize our created purpose.

Understanding Theism 101: The question has been asked (Phillips, Brown and Stonestreet 2008, 1), "Is life worth living, or is it ultimately absurd?" Practicing theists believe life is worth living for reasons beyond personal human experience. This has to do with how we answer several basic worldview questions:

Is there a God? *Yes.*

Is that God personal? *Yes.*

What is the nature of a human being? *Created in God's image with His intent.*

What happens when we die? *We continue to exist in a newer, better way.*

Why do we believe this? *God has revealed His thoughts to us through word and the world, and for biblical theists, through Jesus as well. We believe life is ultimately meaningful.*

This sits in direct opposition to the answers many nontheists would give to these questions. One of my favorites is H. L. Mencken. It seemed like no matter what I majored in in college (psychology, then sociology, then philosophy, then journalism, before finally getting degrees in bus iness management and in psychology again), Mencken was a hero in every field. In his response to Will Durant's (Durant and Middleton 2011) query as to the meaning of life, Mencken summed up his wonderfully candid essay with the following quote: *"What the meaning of human life may be I don't know: I incline to suspect that it has none. All I know about it is that, to me at least, it is very amusing while it lasts."* In addition, he uses much of his essay to rail against a God in which he does not believe. He closes with this: *"When I die, I shall be content to vanish into nothingness. No show, however good, could conceivably be good forever"* (Ibid.).

I wonder why he could see the good in his own fight against God yet not see the good that God intended for him through the fight. By the way, practicing theists have a long history within their sacred texts of fighting with God. He seems to encourage it for honesty's sake. In his demand to be blessed, "Jacob fought with the angel, and the angel was overcome" (U2 1987). Of course, the price of the truth was a lifetime limp. David's poetry recorded in our Psalms is the poetry of a questioning warrior. Theism is not devoid of thought. When our babies die, we scream at God. Then we wait to hear what He says.

Understanding Theism 101: Life is a big deal to theists. We believe that we are not an accident, that we have individual purpose, and that our days are numbered precisely. That is why we get so upset about abortion and end-of-life decisions. We are also very uptight about the continued life of bad people. Ever notice that pro-life folks are almost always for the death penalty, and pro-abortion folks are almost always against the death penalty? Yeah, that one bothers me, too.

Understanding Theism 101: There is a worldview that basically centers on the idea of meaninglessness. It is called nihilism. In nihilism the basic belief is that there are no absolute moral values. A famous nihilist was Fredrich Nietzsche. He felt that to live was to suffer, and to survive was to find some meaning in the suffering. Nihilism generally gets pretty ugly. I've heard nihilists self-describe their reality as a person as a successful virus clinging to a pile of mud.

I HAVE BEEN CREATED IN THE IMAGE OF GOD. IF ANYONE IS IN CHRIST, HE IS A NEW CREATION. THE OLD HAS PASSED AWAY; BEHOLD THE NEW IS COME. I HAVE BEEN CRUCIFIED WITH CHRIST. IT IS NO LONGER I WHO LIVE, BUT CHRIST WHO LIVES IN ME. THE LIFE I NOW LIVE IN THE FLESH I LIVE BY FAITH IN THE SON OF GOD, WHO LOVED ME AND GAVE HIMSELF FOR ME. I PRAISE YOU, FOR I AM FEARFULLY AND WONDERFULLY MADE. WONDERFUL ARE YOUR WORKS; MY SOUL KNOWS IT VERY WELL. THERE IS THEREFORE NOW NO CONDEMNATION FOR THOSE WHO ARE IN CHRIST JESUS. FOR YOU DID NOT RECEIVE THE SPIRIT OF SLAVERY TO FALL BACK INTO FEAR, BUT YOU HAVE RECEIVED THE SPIRIT OF ADOPTION AS SONS, BY WHOM WE CRY, "ABBA FATHER!" NOW YOU ARE THE BODY OF CHRIST, AND EACH ONE OF YOU IS A PART OF IT. BEFORE I FORMED YOU IN THE WOMB I KNEW YOU, BEFORE YOU WERE BORN I SET YOU APART; I APPOINTED YOU AS A PROPHET TO THE NATIONS. YOU ARE A CHOSEN PEOPLE, A ROYAL PRIESTHOOD, A HOLY NATION, GOD'S SPECIAL POSSESSION, THAT YOU MAY DECLARE THE PRAISES OF HIM WHO CALLED YOU OUT FEAR NOT FOR I HAVE REDEEMED HE GAVE HIS ONLY BEGOTTEN SON OF DARKNESS INTO HIS WONDERFUL LIGHT. YOU; I HAVE THAT WHOSOEVER PERISH BUT HAVE ETERNAL LIFE. CHOOSE THIS DAY CALLED YOU BY YOUR FOR ME AND MY HOUSE, WE WILL SERVE THE NAME, YOU ARE AS FOR THE PALM OF MY HAND. FORGIVEN. MINE. BEHOLD I AM A CHILD OF GOD. REDEEMED. I HAVE INSCRIBED YOU I AM WITH YOU BUT WHOM YOU WILL SERVE. BUT THE AGE. FOR I KNOW THE LORD. I HAVE REDEEMED BELIEVES IN HIM SHALL NOT YOU, DECLARES FOR GOD SO LOVED THE WORLD ALWAYS, EVEN TO THE END OF WELFARE AND NOT FOR EVIL, TO GIVE THE PLANS I HAVE FOR YOU A FUTURE AND A HOPE. HE MUST INCREASE. I MUST DECREASE.

This obviously stands in contrast to the biblically theistic view that declares we were fearfully and wonderfully made, knit together in our mothers' wombs, with every day of our lives known to the creator God.

Be nice to nihilists. Lord knows they need it.

Understanding Theism 101: When theists think about the meaning of life, they think about finding meaning in the context of eternity. This is why radicalized theists are so freaking scary, crashing airplanes they are riding in or showing up at places with bombs and guns, willing to die for what they believe.

To be clear, radicalized fringe members of any religious identity should be monitored and disempowered by the group as much as possible. It is not right that these idiots do what they do, but the plain fact of the matter is that we have not had too many bombs set off by the Naturalistic Humanists for Understanding Dream Interpretation (NHUDI, pronounced "Nutty"). If that group actually existed, they would sit around and discuss the meaning behind Robin Williams's movies. Other worldview adherents simply do not feel the need to die for a cause, though they are often willing to die for others.

This is the worst of what theism has to offer. The raw material for understanding meaning and value in life, when combined with a psychotic view of the nature and desire of a vindictive, angry God, is all it takes for somebody to decide they are going make that crazy God happy by killing themselves and others. The afterlife will have a payoff. Or so they think. Normal theists believe God is a whole lot less worried about punishing people and a whole lot more concerned about making His good name known to them.

Understanding Theism 101: Science, philosophy, religion, and crazy Ken the trumpet guy all take a stab at answering the basic question, What is the meaning of life? Theists not only have their thoughts on this, but are also pretty proud of the stuff they come up with. We cheat a little, because we do not have to figure anything out since we have sacred words from God that essentially tell us the answer. It is usually close to this: love God and enjoy Him forever.

The way we answer this question is foundational to our worldview. It is one of the key places where the theistic train runs off the tracks. For instance, I know many professing Christians who answer the question about the meaning of life in decidedly atheistic terms. They often say that the whole thing is about being happy. It is their ultimate goal for their children to be happy. They get divorced because they are unhappy, and God wouldn't want that. In fact, they believe this so strongly that if they are not happy, they believe God is punishing them. It is not theistic to consider that the meaning of life centers on our own happiness. None of the religious writings that are sacred to theists advocate for that.

Understanding Theism 101: Theists believe the meaning of life is bound together with the fact that God created the world, the universe, and us, and that He had a reason or a purpose for doing so. This means that we deduce our meaning of life from God's creative purpose. We believe that if there were no God behind existence, there would be no meaning.

This thought deserves to be challenged, even if it is ultimately true. If there is no God and therefore no afterlife, and if the freak accident of nature has not duplicated what we have here within some other galaxy far, far away, well, one day the sun will burn out and there will be no mind to hold a memory of anything. That is sad and would mean that ultimately life is absurd and meaningless. Albert Camus wrote of the heroic nihilists who struggle with dignity against a disinterested world (The Myth of Sisyphus 1955).

I just think it is difficult to suggest there is no meaning to a little boy waiting anxiously with a ball and glove for his father to come home from work.

Understanding Theism 101: The meaning of life is not forty-two, no matter how charming that answer is (Adams 1979). Forty-two is my waist size, Jackie Robinson's jersey number, and that's about it. Adams's point was that trying to find meaning in life is nonsensical. It is still a good book, but

Adams writes to present a worldview, and it is not theistic. And you just thought he was being silly.

Understanding Theism 101: Biblical theists believe God created every person with a specific intention. We believe He is deeply connected to who we are and what we are about. We believe He not only keeps a running tab on how many hairs we have on our heads, but He knows how many days we have from the moment we are born until the moment we die. He has a plan and a purpose for each one of us, in addition to His general plan that we know Him, love Him, and love others. He wants us to become certain kinds of people and equips us specifically for that purpose by giving us personalities, skills, strengths, and weaknesses. We believe that He does not make mistakes, and that the difficulties of life are part of helping us to find our way.

This is why biblical theists are preachy and teachy about behavior. We want you to find His way for you, rather than your way for yourself.

Understanding Theism 101: Funerals are a difficult reality of the human experience. In America and much of the rest of the world, a funeral service is the great intersection down Theism Boulevard as it crosses Otherviews Lane. Funeral ceremonies are often the domain of the theistic experts, no matter what the deceased's personal worldview was. I have done funerals for families who have never attended a church service, but they find themselves searching out a Christian pastor to help with some things that they intrinsically seem to need.

I do not mean to suggest that this is hypocritical, and I do my best to be of kind service to hurting people. I get more gratitude and appreciation for these services than you might imagine. I always use Psalm 139 in every service I do for somebody I have never met. I have memorized it, and it is a beautiful psalm, written by a grieving parent. It almost is enough to get people to give theism a chance.

Mixed worldviews are always a challenge when it comes to funerals. So often I am led by the instructions of the deceased to make sure that a gospel message is preached. I can always sense the targets of Grandma's concern as they steel themselves for what they know is coming. If you ever find yourself in this situation, please remember that it is an act of love based upon things that your loved one held dearly. Take the challenge to think about it, and be grateful that somebody was thinking about you and not themselves when they prepared for death.

Understanding Theism 101: Biblical theists believe God has a plan for their lives. This plan is something we call "His will." When biblical theists think about God's will for their lives, they get excited because this means He has a purpose for them. If He has a purpose for them, then their lives have meaning if they can discover His will.

When I go in search of God's will for my life, the first part of the discovery process is actually quite simple. There is a thing called God's general will. That is the same for me as it is for you. These are all the expectations that we can read about in the Scriptures, things like loving enemies, keeping our marriage beds pure, and things like that. It is simple in that we do not have to try hard to figure it out, but it is difficult to enact because these commands or expectations often go against our personal desires. But it is like exercise. It prepares us to do the more difficult thing, which is following God's *specific* will for ourselves.

His specific will is usually found by discovering the details of how we are made. Personality profiles, passions, giftings, and experience can direct us. These things lead us toward such things as vocations, marriages (or not), and where we will live. We try to make connections in such areas as prayer, Scripture, circumstances, and wise counsel from trusted people.

A bit of advice: God is always more concerned about right or wrong than He is right or left.

Chapter 14

Theism and History

I s history directed or undirected? We believe history is linear and directed by a sovereign God. It has a beginning and an end. We believe God uses history to express a meta-narrative about Himself and about us.

Understanding Theism 101: Religion is blamed for almost all war. *The Encyclopedia of War* (Phillips and Axelrod 2004) suggests that of the 1,763 wars since the beginning of recorded history, 123, or around 7 percent, can be classified as religious. According to the encyclopedia, a little more than fourteen Americans die in religious wars each year, a little less than we lose from dog bites. Keep in mind that this is the average since 1776. The encyclopedia weighs in at more than ten pounds, so it must be accurate. The digital version weighs twenty-one grams.

Understanding Theism 101: Theists are a bit divided on their summaries of history, and theists are most inclined to summarize history from the middle. Christians and Jewish people essentially believe that God's work can be tracked throughout history in this basic order: First, He created the cosmos and us. Then, we messed it all up, but He has offered a way of redemption. Eventually, He will restore all things, including us. In Islam, Allah is actively working throughout time to ultimately express His will. In both cases, theists are striving to understand, fix, and join the process.

Pantheists would think this is nuts. In their move toward enlightenment and god-consciousness, the last thing they want to do is to understand, fix, and join processes. Pantheists want to let it go. They want the ticking clock of time to fade into a gentle hum of ambient sound until we all get lost in oneness.

Understanding Theism 101: When theists and postmodernists battle, it is often about a very simple but pronounced difference. Theists like to make sense out of the world by understanding facts and their relationship to one another. Postmodernists like to say that the world doesn't make any sense because of the silly view that facts mean something.

To the postmodernist, the theistic argument that our faith can be validated is simply ridiculous. Our personal experience of God is subjective and cannot be shared. Our empirical observations that God is at work in the world are subjective and have no value. Our experts and authorities are subjectively minded and cannot be trusted. Our use of reason or logic to explain our faith is also used by others to deny God, so that measure is subjective as well. If we even seek to use the scientific method to defend our faith, the postmodernist will believe that explanations of scientific data are all plagued by personal biases that make even that method subjective.

So we are just going to have keep tolerating each other as best we can until the day we die. That day might lead to some changed opinions.

Understanding Theism 101: One of the debates that has surrounded the loss of civility within the American political process centers on our big idea of theism. The understanding for more than two hundred years was that our country was founded on Christian principles. The first intellectual argument against this was the idea that certain predominant Founding Fathers were not Christian but were deists, Thomas Jefferson most definitely. Then we began to pile on every single imperfection of our cultural history. Slavery and racism, white privilege, capitalism-driven Pareto problems (you will have to look it up—this is not the place!), imperialistic military, etc., have all become excuses to either deny or condemn theistic roots. Little credit in recent years has been given to moral successes.

The great American experiment of democracy was once considered to be a product of a theistic, God-driven observation that all were created equal. Now America is set forth as an example of the worst that the world has to offer. I guess I'll believe that when people try to swim to Cuba.

IT SEEMED RIGHT AT THE TIME

Understanding Theism 101: Practicing theists believe that history is linear and purposeful. These ideas are distinct from pantheism, which views history as cyclical, and atheism, which sees history as directionless. This might explain what happens at the Thanksgiving table when there is a practicing biblical theist present. We often give thanks for things God has set back to right, and our political and social conversations might trend toward encouraging the whole world to walking lockstep with His purposes. It makes us appear that we have a moral high-handedness. Sorry, just give us more pie. We will usually stop preaching if we have more pie.

Understanding Theism 101: Practicing theists believe that humanity's shared experiences are not undirected chance, but guided by a director. Theists differ as to how much direction that director affords, but we all agree that God is pulling us through to some big purpose. We believe more in providence than accidents. This might explain why we are always thinking there is a purpose in suffering.

Understanding Theism 101: The history of theism is chock-full of the worst marketing ideas possible, especially for a worldview that holds its adherents responsible for advocating for others to accept that worldview. "God loves you! Don't worry about judgment, sin, hell, slavery, misogyny, submissive wives, bigotry, racism, or the Crusades. Just enjoy this Kool-Aid and meet me at Sunday school."

I hope my theistic friends can see the problem here. Our track record, which is essentially a definition of history, is not very good. We cannot change our history and attempt to explain it away with simplistic generalizations (which is all these posts are offering); that is unpalatable.

This is not to say I do not think the ugly history cannot be explained. It can, but it requires a critical and complete examination of all history, not just the theistic part in the story and the nature of humankind, which has a history that is just as bad. The two "isms" that the world is setting forth as the repair order for theistic destruction are socialism and communism. As bad as theistic history is, I would take theism in a philosophical battle against socialism or communism any day.

Understanding Theism 101: Theists have a long history of wanting to conquer the world. This includes expanding boundaries with religiously infused governments. The root of this behavior comes from the belief that the creator of the universe is talking to a particular group of people about His plans to overtake the world. Muslims and Christians have always been land-grabbers, but our Jewish friends not so much. They just want a nice, gated community and for everyone else to stay out.

In the most recent years, we have been less interested in engaging in wars for land and subjects and more interested in influencing people's hearts and minds. But that is hard, so we try to legislate our way into homes, businesses, and communities.

In biblical theism, I advocate for the approach that I believe Christ presented. He said that Caesar's stuff is Caesar's stuff, even while Caesar was unfairly occupying the homes of Jesus's own people. Christ seemed to think that His infiltration of the world was going to come soul by soul, and He did not seem to be concerned about borders and governments. It has long been observed that we cannot legislate morality. We can no more legislate changed hearts.

Understanding Theism 101: Theists, unfortunately, have a long history of shortsightedness. We thought the Crusades were a good idea. We were very late to the table on social reform issues such as slavery and women's rights. However, I want to be very specific and lay the blame for these types of bad press at the feet of those who deserve it: theists in name only.

Practicing theists were often front and center in these battles, and they show up on the right side of history. The history books are replete with stories about theists such as Dietrich Bonhoeffer, William Wilberforce, Mother Teresa, Martin Luther King Jr., and Sojourner Truth. These are some of the greatest human beings who have ever lived, and they and millions like them fought against wrong and evil, even if it came from the church.

We are truly the best and worst of times.

Chapter 15

Theism and How It Defines Our Behavior

The posts in our closing chapter are not gathered according to the questions we used to sift our way through understanding biblical theism. Rather, this chapter serves as a conclusion. Once we determine that we are viewing life and its many components, such as self, family, community, church, and world through a lens, we must consider the implications of our worldview.

A proper understanding of our worldview can be a welcome help to us. It can assist us in making decisions that will lead to steady results. It can provide a framework for our interpretation of events. It will most certainly provide a plumbline for us to establish a constant character that features integrity. It can help us to see what we are supposed to be and what we are to do with ourselves in the context of our lives and relationships.

These final posts are about what we should be and what we could be.

Understanding Theism 101: Biblical theists can either waddle through life like clowns trying to get into a Volkswagen, or they can put their worldview glasses on and walk down the sidewalk of life without tripping over every little thing.

Throughout my theism posts, I have spoken of biblical theism. The biblical part is the distinguisher between Christian theism and all other monotheistic religions. It further distinguishes us from all other worldviews. The biblical part is very particular. We need to know the biblical part. If only there was a book that had that biblical stuff...

Understanding Theism 101: I am a biblical theist. Many of my friends who read and respond to these posts are not theists, and today's essay is not for them, but they may read it if they like.

This post is for those who claim to be biblical theists. When I use the term *practicing theist* in these posts, I am making a distinction between those who know and live the biblical worldview, and those who do not know or live it but still think they are on the team. This is harsh, and rather than being angry, I would rather you just get busy and join the team. You are welcome anytime.

What does that entail? It is simple. Get familiar with the Bible and do what it says.

I am not bragging here, but you need to know something about me. I cannot think of a single day in the last forty years of my life where I have not read the biblical Scriptures, even if it was just a verse or two. Most often it is longer passages and prescribed reading programs where I can make sure that I am looking at the whole thing on a regular basis. Sometimes it is just a text from a friend or, even more often, a text to a friend offering some scriptural hope or promise. I get Scripture from the music I listen to and from the books I choose to read. It might be easier for me because I am a pastor, but I need what Jesus referred to as daily bread. You need it, too.

Understanding Theism 101: Do worldviews shape our political bents? Absolutely, but not entirely. My church is a mix of Republican, Libertarian, Democrat, and "Donotcareitan." Theism very strongly values human dignity, so practicing theists will value human dignity. This will push forward a political agenda that values human dignity. Different experiences will shape how we advocate for that particular value of dignity. For some of us, it is to wholeheartedly support First Amendment rights, and for others, it is to passionately seek to restrain those rights. It is the same for the Second Amendment, abortion, the death penalty, taxes, or any other political platform plank you can imagine.

If you listen to people of any religion or worldview as they push a political agenda, you will hear them plead on behalf of their neighbors, the oppressed, the working class, and children. There is always a concern for others. One side wants gun control because of their concern for others. The other side wants the right to bear arms so their neighbors can be safe from threat. The love for others is our common political ground. If we could just appreciate that in our discussions, we might be able to take advantage of the amazing common ground of love and get some things done without all the acrimony.

By the way, the right to "bare arms" is an appeal to the freedom to wear sleeveless shirts. But the tattoo was beautiful.

Understanding Theism 101: As we emerge from two years of world-wide pandemic, many theists are coming down on one of two sides in the WWJDDAPTHHFM ("what would Jesus do during a pandemic to help his fellow man," in case you didn't know) debate. One side says that we love our neighbor by protecting them from viruses...or vaccines. Dang—one side of the debate, two groups already. Anyway, the other side feels that we love our neighbor best by conquering fears and limitations and going boldly into virus-infected airplanes mask free. There are variations, but each side is theistically interested in their neighbor's well-being. Each side can make a claim to Scripture, and each side can take the moral high ground. This is one of the most beautiful aspects of theism, particularly biblical theism: the paradoxical nature of loyally following Christ or sacred texts down a path different from the one of a faithful friend. A wonderful illustration of this is found in the movie *The Mission* (Joffe 1986). I highly suggest you watch for early Liam Neeson as a Jesuit priest.

Understanding Theism 101: You would think some families have a magic force in their homes that makes them fight with each other. They seek counseling, hoping to get past some things so they do not have to fight all the time.

Theists believe that if we fight with someone, it is because we want to fight with them, or at the very least, we do not want to *not* fight with them. We believe that loving others, not yelling at others and not demanding our own way with others, is a choice we can make because we have been endowed with free will. We are not victims of the magic-fight-club force. So just stop it.

Understanding Theism 101: A little Facebook observation: Many of us Christian types enjoy the opportunities Facebook provides to do at least two things: offer praise and glory to God, and complain that the rest of the world does not do the same. It makes for interesting conversations when worldviews collide. I will offer a few things that nontheists should remember about their theistic friends.

First, practicing theists are aware of the difference between the ideal and the "really are." By this I mean we often make statements about the faith-life that we are simply aspiring to, not claiming we have reached.

Second, of all the worldviews, theism, especially biblical theism, is the only one bound to warn their neighbors, whether they want to hear it or not, that we do not get a free pass into the afterlife. We believe we will all be judged after we die. It is irritating, but we really believe it.

Third, practicing theists are big on putting things back to right. It all flows out of the personal Creator stuff that we believe in so deeply. Sometimes our hearts' beliefs are more vivid than our ability to communicate.

Fourth, a quote from Churchill, who stole it from Don Marquis: "An idea is not responsible for those who believe in it" (quotes.net 2014). Gandhi said it nicely, as well: "I like Christianity, not so much Christians" (Harvard Crimson 2020) Some of us are extremely poor examples of the ideal, both in speech and action. Some of the worst of us are also the most enthusiastic.

Understanding Theism 101: One of the overarching themes in biblical theism is the story that God wants us to know and experience peace. Peace is often abandoned by muddle-headed theists who are in pursuit of a human-istic goal called happiness. Happiness is not bad, but in theism it is rarely encouraged to be a goal worth pursuing. As practicing theists, we will always be aware of those moments when we realize that our unhappiness is causing us to push away from theistic values. When we catch ourselves, we are obli-gated to reorient our thinking toward other pursuits, such as righteous-ness, humility, and peacefulness. Happiness is not a virtue. Peacemaking is a virtue. Humility is a virtue. Righteousness is a virtue. Happiness is some-thing you feel as the product of good fortune, all the way from an ice cream cone to marrying the person of your dreams. You are not a virtuous person because you are experiencing happiness.

However, if you pursue virtues rather than feelings or stuff, you might just experience more happiness than you would otherwise. It is not a promise, but it is likely. So many wrong things can bring happiness, but we all know how fleeting that can be.

Biblical theists know that you pay for virtue growth in cold, hard cash. You read and study and practice and fail, but as the virtue grows into your character, it is bought and paid for. People who seek happiness without virtue are paying on credit. There will be a price to pay. It might be debt, a headache, or even a divorce.

Chase virtue in your life. Happiness might just catch you from behind.

Understanding Theism 101: Practicing theists in the United States believe that their gratitude during the Thanksgiving holiday, and every day, is directed toward a personal God. Gratitude is a little different from thankfulness. I am sure some of us appear to be lunatics, looking for silver linings during gray days. It has a lot to do with the fact that practicing theists do not pursue happiness, but chase after peace. At least we are supposed to, and Thanksgiving reminds us of that.

Understanding Theism 101: Do you love your spouse? Do you love your children? Do you love the poor in Bangladesh or on the street corners of your hometown? Do you love chocolate cake?

We often use the word *love* when what we really mean is *likes a lot*. What do we mean when we talk about love? I know some people who love their girlfriends the same way I love burritos. I love a burrito for what it provides for me, for the way it makes me feel while I am devouring it. When a burrito no longer provides me with anything beyond a good memory, I am on to looking for the next burrito. Is that how you want to be loved? Is that how you love?

At my church, we talk about love in decidedly unromantic, unfeeling terms. We say, "Love is meeting needs," specifically, the needs of others to be safe, significant, and accepted. Romance is cool and exciting, but it is only the gravy on the chicken-fried steak of life. I must be hungry right now.

My friend Nick quotes author Gary Thomas, saying, Dating does not prepare us for marriage. Dating prepares us for vacations." (Melazzo 2019). Love is something we do, not a description of something we feel.

I listen as a fellow tells me he just doesn't love his wife anymore. I know he is telling me about how he is feeling. Anybody with two eyes can see he doesn't love her just by looking at how he speaks to her and treats her. I have another friend who talks about his wife all the time. He is always positive, always admiring, always thinking of ways to serve her. She has dementia and is getting further and further away from even remembering who he is, but he loves her.

I know these thoughts are not limited to Christianity. But I also know these thoughts are foundational to the teaching of Christ. We talk about these things on Sunday mornings.

Understanding Theism 101: Practicing Christians follow the example of Christ. The fourth chapter of the book of Matthew summarizes what Christ went about doing, namely, preaching, teaching, and performing kind acts. There were some miracles, but mostly just conversations and service to those who needed a break. Christians get off track and become really irritating to normal people when they focus their following on only one or two of the examples of Christ. We preach because we believe the bridge is out and the only way to avoid a tragic loss is to choose to follow the one who knows the way—Jesus. We teach because we believe good choices lead to good consequences. The most significant of these consequences is peace, of which Christ is called, "Prince." We serve because we love, and love will be the ruling ethos once the kingdom of God reigns fully, which we believe it one day will.

I think our motivation looks much different from this to most normal people. I think they see us preach to express hatred. I think they see us teach to express arrogance. I think they often see us serve to express fear, weakness, or capitulation. I believe that unless they see us serve sacrificially and in love, they will not hear us preach and teach. I think that if they see us serve but we fail to preach and teach, we are not fully committed to the example of Christ.

Understanding Theism 101: Practicing theists may drive people crazy with their rules and religious intolerance, but theists of all religious expressions can be incredibly generous with their personal finances. This is not to say that people from other worldview perspectives are not generous. They often are. Theists typically understand that as God is the creator and sustainer of all things, everything, including money, ultimately belongs to Him. This brings a factor called stewardship into play. We tend to understand that we only manage God's money. As such, most practicing theists give a portion of their income to their church, synagogue, or mosque. In addition, they tend to give beyond that to ministries or causes they support. Many biblical theists will give their vacation time and money to work in filthy slums or in a third-world hospital. Again, one does not have to be a theist to do these things, but theists do it a lot. I have been overseas with well more than two hundred different people who just want to help somewhere. It is one of our best things.

Understanding Theism 101: Theists are among the few worldview adherents who organize according to their worldview. Pantheists do, and sometimes angry atheists do, but theists really get into it. We get up early to do things related to our worldview. Last Saturday I had pumpkin pancakes and held hands with a group of at least fifteen male biblical theists. We didn't call it a male biblical theists' early Saturday food gathering. We called it a prayer breakfast. This might help explain why we tend to be so political and have so many coalitions.

Understanding Theism 101: Last night I listened to my friend and mentor, Max Barnett, share a talk on prayer with a castle-full of university students from throughout the Midwest. We were at a conference in beautiful Glen Eyrie in Colorado Springs. My particular theistic bent, as you are aware, is biblical, Protestant, non-Reformed, Baptist, etc., but I tried very hard to listen to Max's talk as an outsider. As Max began to share his ten reasons why God might not be answering our prayers, I could see that a nontheist would likely have received his thoughts very well. Max is in his seventies and is a straight shooter with a wealth of knowledge and outstanding communication skills. If I were a nontheist listening to Max, I think I would have concluded that hope and faith are more mature and less childish than commonly thought. I would have conceded that a thorough understanding of Scripture reveals a much more coherent idea of God than the silly genie-in-the-sky-granting-wishes-for-his-minions kind of dude that antagonists to the theistic worldview claim for us. I might have thought I was watching Brainwashing 101 in action at the way hundreds of university students were hanging on every word he said, but Max is sort of a hero to our type of person.

All of that aside, as I listened as an outsider to what Max shared with the students, I got a little misty-eyed. I love that old man. He moves me. I imagine he presents an intellectual, emotional, and spiritual earthquake for a person from another worldview. There is something to be said for the person who lives out their worldview in a steady way over the course of a lifetime who has been rewarded with peace. Max is reasonable and highly educated, yet it is his life that is his better argument for the faith.

Understanding Theism 101: Practicing theists believe in a personal God, and by personal I mean a God with identity, personality, and character qualities. Based on these character qualities, we believe we are endowed with three uniquely human functions: (1) ethical thought, (2) the ability to reason, and (3) the ability to develop and maintain personal relationships with other people and with God. These beliefs bring form to our understanding of several key worldview questions: How do we know right from wrong? How do we know anything at all? What is a person?

These core beliefs about the character of God and subsequent placement of these qualities into His creation explain a few things about theists. It gives a little insight as to why there are no sign-up sheets for PETA in church bulletins. It speaks to why we worry about righteousness and sin. It brings understanding to our continual reference to fellowship and forgiveness.

Understanding Theism 101: I'm going to throw down a few theistic showstoppers against some of the favorite advice the world offers. The "world" is what biblical theists call anybody but themselves, for your information. How do theists feel about the idea of YOLO, as expressed by building-jumpers and shark-wrestlers? "You only live once" is the battle cry of those bravely and fiercely deciding to not go gentle into that good night. The sentiment is understandable if not even admirable. The problem is that it is also stupid in a risk/reward scenario. The reason people have subscribed to YOLO as a life guide is because they do not believe anything could be more significant than a chemical reaction in their bodies. Adrenaline is not much different from meth if it becomes your highest goal.

Theists also believe in YOLO, but in a different context. We believe in YOLOBYDITM. That is pronounced "yolobiddittum," and it means you only live once but you die in the middle. That puts a huge twist in the philosophy. I call dibs on the band name.

Understanding Theism 101: Let us see if theism has another mic drop in the philosophic battle of idioms. Theists often appreciate the Latin dictum of carpe diem. It means to seize the day in a world where we let so much go by and where we become dull to the ever-ticking clock. Carpe diem is an appeal to enjoy life today because tomorrow is not guaranteed. It literally means to spend today rather than save for the future.

The theistic approach is much more akin to two awesome book titles by Christian authors. Len Sweet wrote *Carpe Manana* (2001) in an effort to encourage biblical theists to let easy wins today go by in order that they might lay groundwork for great wins tomorrow, especially within the context of church leadership. This is reminiscent of Solomon's ants from the book of Proverbs. Erwin McManus wrote *Seizing Your Divine Moment* (2002) to encourage us not to miss chances for greatness by enjoying the moment. He shared a great story of his carpe diem day on the beach when he let his pastoral heart lie in submission to a vacation moment as he conveniently ignored a blind man struggling to find his way through the crowd. Suddenly his preteen son seized the divine moment, ran to the man, and helped him find his way. There was gratitude, joy, and appreciation from others who saw selflessness and sacrifice in his boy. Theists who are doing it right are going to seize divine moments.

Understanding Theism 101: Another day, another philosophy battle featuring theists against the world. This one is kind of fun because with this particular maxim, the typical nontheist is actually invoking the nature of God in their argument. Do you know what is coming?

God loves me just the way I am. Now, to be fair, it is more often that this argument is presented by a nominal or former theist. It is presented in writing most often by tattoo artists. The argument that God loves me just the way I am is designed to justify character issues or to get the holier-than-thou types off some poor guy's back. It is used to express the hope that surely God is not as judgmental as all these theists are.

Well, in biblical theism, God does love me just the way I am. That is great news. The even better news? He loves me too much to let me stay this way. The even-better-than-that news? He provided a way for me to be changed into a new creation. That is called the good news of the gospel, by the way. The really bad news, and the reason we get nervous with this axiom, is that if we deny God's gift to make ourselves right, we can't make it into heaven.

Yep. This one scares a theist.

Understanding Theism 101: How about another matchup in the theism versus the world's-best-advice series. A lot of T-shirts and baseball caps tell me to follow my heart. Some tinkly-poo songs add in that my heart will never lead me astray. How do theists feel about this wholesome, self-actualized ideal?

They feel exactly the same way anybody with a brain feels about this advice. It is stupid and almost always leads to an unhappy life.

Do theists think the heart is evil? Well, first we better decide what we mean when we use the word. Most of us would agree that we are speaking of hopes and desires and wishes that are centered on our best outcomes. In itself, that is not really evil. It may be a bit selfish, but if nobody else is harmed, it's not that bad, right? Right. Except, unless you are the luckiest S.O.B. who ever lived, you are not going to get what you wish for. It only happens in movies, and that is why we pay fifteen bucks to see the dream come true for some actress who in real life is on the sixth love of her life this year.

In biblical theism, our text warns us that following our heart is foolishness. Our brains are not even good enough. God says to follow His commands and He will take care of the rest.

One thing is for sure. Facebook is a lot more fun because of the people who follow their hearts, if you are a sadist and enjoy that sort of thing.

Understanding Theism 101: I am having fun with theism versus the world. Tonight's matchup: theism versus "you are beautiful just the way you are."

No, you are not. Before you get sad, let me remind you that absolutely nobody makes the cover of *Vogue* without paint and Photoshop. Also, let us not pretend that the sentiment behind this statement is about the idea that beauty is about something other than simple physical beauty. I think people already know and understand what real beauty is, but that is not what this idiom is advocating. I could live with this axiom if it were saying that we are valuable just the way we are. Theists *should* believe that any physical beauty is fleeting. Flaunting that beauty is vain and cheap. We *should* believe that what we would like others to see most brightly in us is what we are seeing first in them. But theists fall for the lie about physical beauty as quickly as anyone else, and we contribute to one of the most successful markets in the capitalistic first world—body morphing.

There is so much unhappiness, and it is championed by queens of eating disorders and kings of weight room narcissism. In a few years, the new kings and queens roll in and the old ones are rolled over, and the parade continues in front of admiring masses.

The actual theistic counter to this saying is probably something like Pedro said in *Napoleon Dynamite*: "Vote for Jesus, and your wildest dreams will come true" (Ramirez 2004). Okay, maybe that is not quite what he said, but it is better. If we can only trust the plan of the Creator, there will come a day when our appearance and health will be completely awesome. And it will hardly matter to us by then.

Theists need to rally around what we really believe about beauty. It is a condition of the cared-for soul rather than the pampered and promoted body part. I would refer you to the stories of two biblical theists who learned this in the most wondrously difficult ways. Nick Vujicic, the man born with no arms and legs, and Lizzie Velasquez, who was born with a disease that earned her the cruel internet title of the ugliest woman in the world. Google them. Listen to their stories to learn what beautiful really is. It is agreeing with God about our worth in His eyes.

I believe in beautiful souls.

Understanding Theism 101: Another philosophy showdown: Theism takes on revenge!

Revenge is a dish best served cold. Get even or die trying. Settle the score. All these bits of advice flow from the same concept, that when you have been harmed by others, you must become dedicated to take vengeance upon your enemies.

Biblical theism is particularly set against the idea of revenge. There are a couple of steady reasons why we do not advocate for vengeance. One reason is that holding dreams of revenge also causes us to hold resentment within our hearts, our minds, and our souls. Resentment is like sour cream. You can even use all the same letters in *sour cream* to spell resentment. Please tell me you did not just try to do that. Anyway, resentment is like sour cream in that it goes rotten and smells horrific if something is not done with it very soon. Harbored bitterness is a "stinkfest." Most of us never actually get to pull off revenge anywhere other than in our dreams. The ones who do ply their revenge are often arrested, or even worse, their enemy doubles up and does them in again.

Another reason theists should be able to let go of revenge and take another slap across the cheek is that God promises us that in the end He will avenge us, and that He will attend to things so severely that we will despair even for our enemies.

For biblical theists, a willingness to lay down our right to revenge, trusting that God will bless us by taking our burden and pain, comes with a promise of comfort. I have a friend named Tim who lost his twenty-year-old daughter to a drunk driver more than a decade ago. He learned that his only path to peace was to give his anger and his need for revenge to God to let Him redeem this story. Now a man who was nothing more than a scum killer drunk driver is not called that anymore. He is called Henry, and Tim is his friend.

The biggest reason that biblical theists do not support the idea of vengeance is because we believe that each one of us is as guilty as the next guy when it comes to being square with God. He tells us that if we cannot forgive the other guy for his harm against us, He cannot forgive us. And this puts us in our place.

Understanding Theism 101: One more event in the theism-versus-philosophies-of-the-world debate. I heard a father tell his teenage boy this one time: "You gotta do what's best for yourself." That one is advice that comes from someone who has learned the hard way that most of the world is operating from the same viewpoint. A little self-protection is a good thing, but theists, especially biblical theists, must temper this advice with what they know from Scripture. The Bible advises us to look out for the needs of others and to sacrifice our comfort on behalf of others, whether they are poor or rich. Yep, that is the Sermon on the Mount.

This seems to be counterintuitive to our best interests. Well, that depends upon whether we want our best interests to be met by ourselves or by an all-knowing, all-loving, almighty God.

Understanding Theism 101: Not only are there three major religions within theism but within each religion, there are multiple expressions. That makes it hard to generalize about the specific question of, What is God going to do about "fill in the blank"? The Supreme Court ruling of yesterday regarding the cake/no cake issue, features three basic responses being thrown around by theists: Thus, saith the Lord, "I will fry the LGBTQ community, and NASCAR fans, too." Or, thus saith the Lord, "I will fry the judgmental hypocrites who get up early on Sundays for lodge meetings, and NASCAR fans, too." And, thus saith the Lord, "What Supreme Court ruling? Stop bothering me. I have to fry NASCAR fans."

Let me slip my own thoughts into this, thoughts that are sifted through the sieve of theism, then Christianity, then Western culture, specifically American Midwest 1960's born and bred, then Southern Baptist but admittedly not the lockstep kind, and with a giant touch of influence much more by U2 than by John Calvin. God loves sinners but hates sin. I am admitting my bias.

Again—God loves sinners but hates sin. It seems like my preacher friends sometimes forget that God loves sinners. Will He welcome them with open arms? Literally, I believe He will welcome them with arms nailed open. My hippie friends sometimes forget that God hates sin. Will He allow it into His presence? No. Not even a tiny bit. I agree with Oswald Chambers (My Utmost for His Highest 1935), who felt that the greatest evidence of God's respect for humanity is that He allows us to choose against Him, even if it means we walk away from His presence for all eternity. Before you agree this is a good idea, remember that He is *all* good, and *all* good is contained within Him. Basically, I am saying that God does not send people to hell. He saves us from hell. But our sin has to burn. We do not get to take it with us.

So, preacher friends, celebrate the love for humanity that the hippies have. It is truly Christlike. Hippie friends, sit in awe of the warning from the preachers. It is also Christlike, because Christ Himself reminds us, "If it was all about being nice, I would not have had to die. I had to die to pay the price for your sin. If you don't trade your sin for My love, if you still want your way instead of My way, My open arms mean nothing to you."

So, from this long post we can learn two things: theists capitalize personal pronouns referencing God, and NASCAR fans need to switch to baseball.

Appendix

How Various Worldviews Answer the Basic Questions

Theism (Christianity, including Catholicism and extrabiblical religions; Judaism; and Islam)

1) Is reality knowable or unknowable? *Knowable.*

2) Do you believe in a god or gods? *One God with personality.*

3) Do you believe in the supernatural? *Definitely. God is beyond nature.*

4) Where do you think stuff came from? *God made it.*

5) What do you believe about the nature of time? *There was a beginning of time and there will be an end. Eternity exists outside of time.*

6) What is a human being? *A purposeful creation of God that somehow contains elements of God's personality. Life began only once, thousands of years ago when God breathed life into man, and life is passed on, life unto life.*

7) What happens to us when we die? *We continue to exist. We face a judgment, heaven or hell.*

8) How do we know right from wrong? *Partially from observing natural law, mostly from revealed law (Bible, Qur'an, or Torah). Our moral compass is external, not internal.*

9) What is evil? *Ruined good. Evil is a consequence of not following God's plan for us.*

10) How do we know anything at all? *Created nature and time provide an environment for us to connect with God.*

11) What is the meaning and purpose of life? *To connect with and to be made right by God. To recognize our created purpose.*

12) Is history directed or undirected? *It is directed by a sovereign God. It is linear, but without beginning or end. Time is contained within, like eternity is the paper on which the finite timeline is drawn. History is meant to reveal the solution to our individual and corporate search for God.*

Naturalistic Atheism

1) Is reality knowable or unknowable? *Knowable.*

2) Do you believe in a god or gods? *None.*

3) Do you believe in the supernatural? *No. Nature is all we have.*

4) Where do you think stuff came from? *The big bang. Matter must have always existed in some form or other.*

5) What do you believe about the nature of time? *It always existed.*

6) What is a human being? *An evolutionary development. Individual human beings have no special inherent value beyond the fact that they have conscious awareness.*

7) What happens to us when we die? *Oblivion.*

8) How do we know right from wrong? *Observation and evolved social conditioning and constructs.*

9) What is evil? *Bad fortune that could happen at the same statistical rate to anyone.*

10) How do we know anything at all? *Scientific method, reason.*

11) What is the meaning and purpose of life? *Ultimately, there is no meaning, but individual meaning might be extrapolated.*

12) Is history directed or undirected? *Undirected. The evolutionary law of survival of the fittest rules. It is linear, without beginning and end.*

Humanistic Atheism

1) Is reality knowable or unknowable? *Knowable, and God does not exist.*

2) Do you believe in a god or gods? *None.*

3) Do you believe in the supernatural? *Yes, but only to explain pseudo-spiritual concepts such as love and romance or metaphysical visions. A greater emphasis is placed upon the chance that beyond all hope we have come to be alive, and that the evolutionary process has given us an opportunity to self-actualize, at least for a while.*

4) Where do you think stuff came from? *The big bang. Matter must have always existed in some form or other. It can be subjective, or it can be objective.*

5) What do you believe about the nature of time? *It always existed. It is a string of events that are a series of causes leading to effects, leading to causes, and so on.*

6) What is a human being? *An evolutionary development. Individual human beings have no special inherent value beyond the fact that they have conscious awareness. Human beings hold the ultimate value of all evolved realities, and conscious choices help us to rise above the trivial. Humans make themselves to be who they are. We literally define our existence.*

7) What happens to us when we die? *Oblivion. Death is absurd.*

8) How do we know right from wrong? *Observation and evolved social conditioning and constructs.*

9) What is evil? *Bad fortune that could happen at the same statistical rate to anyone.*

10) How do we know anything at all? *From a combination of scientific method, reason, and self-awareness from which we must revolt in order to create value on our own terms.*

11) What is the meaning and purpose of life? *An evolutionary process has produced mankind from nothingness, and while we are here, we are obligated to add our stories to the evolving story of mankind. There is ultimately no purpose in life beyond the purpose we extract from our existence.*

12) Is history directed or undirected? *It is directed by intentional interaction with time and chance, but ultimately, it is without purpose.*

Agnosticism

1) Is reality knowable or unknowable? *Knowable, but with a clear distinction that the supernatural is unknowable.*

2) Do you believe in a god or gods? *This is not something we can determine. Human reason and observation are incapable of providing sufficient rational grounds to justify either the belief that God exists or the belief that God does not exist. If God does exist, He is irrelevant.*

3) Do you believe in the supernatural? *We believe in the possibility of the supernatural, but it is impossible to know for sure what, if anything, is beyond nature. The only thing that can be tested for sure is the natural.*

4) Where do you think stuff came from? *Personal, empirical, and scientific evidence can direct our understanding. Theories that are not provable by the scientific method can never be more than a theory. Since we cannot prove the beginning of the universe, we cannot be sure where everything came from.*

5) What do you believe about the nature of time? *It probably always existed.*

6) What is a human being? *Most likely an evolutionary development. We have limited knowledge.*

7) What happens to us when we die? *We do not know.*

8) How do we know right from wrong? *Observation and evolved social conditioning and constructs.*

9) What is evil? *It is a reality that we know by observation and experience.*

10) How do we know anything at all? *From a combination of scientific method, reason, and self-awareness.*

11) What is the meaning and purpose of life? *It is a process that has produced mankind from nothingness, and while we are here, we are obligated to add our stories to the story of mankind.*

12) Is history directed or undirected? *It is directed by intentional interaction with time and chance.*

Transcendentalism (Buddhism, Hinduism, Taoism, Scientology, Wicca, New Age, Unitarianism, Pantheism, Panentheism, Animism, American Transcendentalism)

1) Is reality knowable or unknowable? *Knowable, and spiritual. Reality is secondary to the spiritual realm, which is the primary reality. The natural world is a platform to engage with the supernatural.*

2) Do you believe in a god or gods? *God is generally an impersonal force, but transcendental religions are all over the map in how we name and identify certain aspects or characteristics of God. We are an extension of the divine nature of God.*

3) Do you believe in the supernatural? *The supernatural is our primary reality, and transcendence away from the natural into the supernatural is our primary goal.*

4) Where do you think stuff came from? *The essence or soul of every living being is one and the same as the essence or soul of the cosmos.*

5) What do you believe about the nature of time? *Time is not real. The goal of every life is to realize that we are one with everything. This enlightenment allows us to pass beyond time.*

6) What is a human being? *Each person is "god," but a lack of awareness makes it difficult for us to move from individual personal identities to become an impersonal reality.*

7) What happens to us when we die? *Death is the end of individual existence. Some religions believe we will be reincarnated until we get it right; others believe death is a shortcut to the end.*

8) How do we know right from wrong? *The more we recognize our oneness with the universe, the farther beyond good and evil we pass. The cosmos is perfection.*

9) What is evil? *It is an illusion.*

10) How do we know anything at all? *By becoming less concerned with what we know and more concerned with our oneness with the cosmos.*

11) What is the meaning and purpose of life? *It is a process that allows us to lose ourselves into the oneness of the cosmos. It is a chance to deny the essence of reality.*

12) Is history directed or undirected? *It is directing all things toward ultimate oneness.*

Bibliography

Achenbach, Joel. 2013. "Achenblog." *Washington Post Online*. May 14. Accessed August 15, 2016. http://www.washingtonpost.com/blogs/achenblog/wp/2013/05/14/why-theres-something-rather-than-nothing/.

Adams, Douglas. 1979. *The Hitchhikers Guide to the Galaxy*. London: Pan Books.

Adhererents.com. 2015. "Major Branches." *Adherents.com*. March 5. Accessed March 30, 2022. http://adherents.com/branches_by_adh.html.

Aquinas, Thomas. 1948. *The Summa Theologica of Saint Thomas Aquinas, English Translation*. Notre Dame, IN: Christian Classics.

Asma, Stephen T. 2010. "Green Guilt." *The Chronicle of Higher Education*. January 10. Accessed May 10, 208. https://www.chronicle.com/article/green-guilt/.

2009. *Does God Exist? William Lane Craig vs. Christopher Hitchens*. Directed by Biola.

Bonhoeffer, Dietrich. 1966. *The Cost of Discipleship*. New York City: Macmillon.

Bono. 2022. ""Last Night on Earth"." *U2.com*. May 20. https://www.u2.com/music/lyrics/76/.

Brain, Marshall. 2012. *Why Won't God Heal Amputees*. December 12. Accessed September 14, 2014. http://whywontgodhealamputees.com/.

Camus, Albert. 1955. *The Myth of Sisyphus*. New York: Alfred A Knoph, Inc.

1946. *It's a Wonderful Life.* Directed by Frank Capra.

Chambers, Oswald. 1935. *My Utmost for His Highest.* London: Dodd, Mead and Company.

Colson, Charles. 1976. *Born Again.* Grand Rapids, Michigan: Baker Publishing.

1998. *The Waterboy.* Directed by Frank Coraci.

Cumming, Jack. 2008. *William Lane Craig vs. Peter Atkins.* June 26. Accessed December 28, 2019. https://www.bing.com/videos/search?q=william+lane+craig+peter+atkins&docid=6079933459187175448&mid=5196C119583476D6405C-5196C119583476D6405C&view=detail&FORM=VIRE.

2016. "Definition of science in English." *lexico.com.* April 16. https://www.lexico.com/en/definition/science.

Durant, Will, and Owen C. Middleton. 2011. *On the Meaning of Life.* Whitefish, Montana: Literary Licensing, LLC.

Ecklund, Elaine Howard. 2010. *Science vs. Religion: What scientists really think.* New York: Oxford.

Editors. 2012. *500 Questions about God and Christianity.* December 12. Accessed September 14, 2014. http://500questions.wordpress.com/.

EQ Staff. 2022. "13 Examples of Natural Laws." *EQxamples.* March 23. https://www.exampleslab.com/13-examples-of-natural-laws/.

Faulkner, William. 1929. *The Sound and the Fury.* Cape and Harrison.

FEVAministries. 2011. "Worldview Summary." *visualunit.files.wordpress.com.* Accessed October 3, 2015. https://visualunit.files.wordpress.com/2011/10/worldview_summary.pdf.

1988. *Indiana Jones and the Last Crusade.* Directed by Steven Spielberg. Performed by Harrison Ford.

2004. *Passion of the Christ, The.* Directed by Mel Gibson. Performed by Mel Gibson.

Gilbert, Elizabeth. 2006. *Eat, Pray, Love: One Woman's Search for Everything Across Italy, India and Indonesia.* New York City: Penguin.

Harper, Jennifer. 2012. "84 percent of the world population has faith; a third are Christian." *The Washington Post.* December 23. Accessed December 30, 2019. https://www.washingtontimes.com/blog/watercooler/2012/dec/23/84-percent-world-population-has-faith-third-are-ch/.

Harvard Crimson. 2020. "MAHATMA GANDHI SAYS HE BELIEVES IN CHRIST BUT NOT CHRISTIANITY." *Harvard Crimson.* Accessed June 12, 2022. https://www.thecrimson.com/article/1927/1/11/mahatma-gandhi-says-he-believes-in/.

Hawking, Stephen. 1998. *A Brief History of Time, 10th Edition.* New York, N.Y.: Bantam Doubleday Dell Publishers.

Hawking, Stephen, and Leonard Mlodinow. 2010. *The Grand Design.* London, England: Bantam Press.

Heflick, Nathan A. 2018. *(A)theism, Meaning, and Death Anxiety.* March 13. https://www.psychologytoday.com/us/blog/the-big-questions/201803/atheism-meaning-and-death-anxiety#:~:text=As%20such%2C%20it%20appears%20that%20at%20an%20explicit,have%20more%20of%20an%20impact%20reducing%20death%20anxiety.

Heschel, A.J. 1955. *God in Search of Man.* New York: Unknown.

2006. *Nacho Libre.* Directed by Jered Hess.

Hurley, Maurice. 1989. "Star Trek The Next Generation: Q-Who." Bowman, Rob, May 8.

1986. *The Mission.* Directed by Roland Joffe.

Keller, Timothy K. 2019. *Sermons.* March 11. Accessed March 16, 2022. https://podcast.gospelinlife.co.

Krailsheimer, A. J. 1966. *Pascal's Pensees.* New York, N.Y.: Penguin Putnam, Inc.

Kreeft, Peter. 1982. *Between Heaven and Hell.* Downers Grove, Illinois: InterVarsity Press.

Kren. 2006. "Why Do People Believe in God." *Way of the Mind.* September 28. Accessed June 30, 2014. http://www.wayofthemind.org/2006/09/27/why-do-people-believe-in-god.

Kumar, Varun. 2020. "Origin of the universe: Seven different theories." *Rankred.com.* September 10. Accessed March 22, 2022. https://www.rankred.com/origin-of-the-universe-different-theories/.

LeBerge, Carmen. 2022. *How to test a worldview.* April 16. Accessed April 16, 2022. https://reconnectwithcarmen.com/how-to-test-a-worldview/?msclkid=e7cce1a8bdc211eca344dd4fd77f353a.

Lennox, John C. 2011. *God and Stephen Hawking; Whose design is it anyway?* Oxford, England: Lion Hudson plc.

Lewis, C. S. 1970. *God in the Dock: Essays on Theology and Ethics.* United Kingdom: Eerdmans.

—. 1952, renewed 1980. *Mere Christianity.* New York, N.Y.: Harper Collins Publishers.

—. 1974-reprint. *Miracles.* London, England: Fontana.

—. 1955. *Surprised by Joy.* New York: Harcourt Brace.

Lewis, C.S. 1945. *The Great Divorce.* London: Geoffrey Bles.

London, Jack. 1903, republished 1982. *The Call of the Wild.* New York City, NY: Pengun Books.

2007. *Big Bang Theory.* Directed by Chuck Lorre and Bill Prady.

1977. *Star Wars.* Directed by George Lucas.

Luck, Kenny. 2014. "Sexual Atheism: Christian Dating Data Reveals a Deeper Spiritual Malaise." *Christian Post.* April 10. Accessed May 22, 2015. https://www.christianpost.com/news/sexual-atheism-christian-dating-data-reveals-a-deeper-spiritual-malaise.html.

Marquis, Don. 2021. "Quotes." *Good Reads.* November 6. https://www.goodreads.com/quotes/1157661-an-idea-isn-t-responsible-for-the-people-who-believe-in.

1987. *Ishtar.* Directed by Elaine May.

McDowell, Josh. 1999. *The New Evidence That Demands a Verdict: Fully Updated to Answer the Questions Challenging Christians Today.* Nashville, TN: Word Publishers.

McManus, Erwin R. 2002. *Seizing Your Divine Moment: Dare to live a life of adventure.* Nashville: Thomas Nelson.

Melazzo, Nick. 2019. "Personal conversation." Grand Junction, Colorado, January 3.

Metaxas, Eric. 2010. *Bonhoeffer: Pastor, prophet, martyr, spy.* Nashville, Tennessee : Thomas Nelson, Inc.

Morison, Frank. 1930. *Who Moved the Stone?* London: Faber and Faber Ltd.,.

1997. *Austin Powers: International Man of Mystery.* Directed by Jay Roach. Performed by Michael Myers.

Needtobreathe. 2014. *More Heart, Less Attack.* Cond. Bear Rinehart. Comps. Bear Rinehart and Bo Rinehart.

Pascal, Blaise, and W.F. (translator) Trotter. 2002. "Pensées." *NTSLibrary.* July 10. Accessed April 22, 2015. http://www.ccel.org/ccel/pascal/pensees.html.

Patowary, Kaushik. 2020. "Thagomizer: Why Stegosaurus' Spiky Tail Was Named After A Cartoon." *Amusing Planet.* July 13. Accessed November 12, 2021. https://www.amusingplanet.com/2020/07/thagomizer-why-stegosaurus-spiky-tail.html.

Peckham, Hannah. 2012. *You don't have a soul. You are a soul. You have a body.* July 5. Accessed May 9, 2017. https://mereorthodoxy.com/you-dont-have-a-soul-cs-lewis-never-said-it/.

2017. *45 Minutes on a single paragraph of Nietzche's Beyond Good and Evil.* Directed by Jordan B Peterson.

Peterson, Jordan B. 2021. *Beyond Order: 12 More Rules for Life.* New York: Penguin.

Phillips, Charles, and Alan Axelrod. 2004. *Encyclopedia of War.* Facts on File.

Phillips, W. Gary, William E. Brown, and John Stonestreet. 2008. *Making Sense of Your World: A biblical worldview.* Salem, Wisconsin: Sheffield Publishing Company.

quotes.net. 2014. *Don Marquis Quotes.* February 12. Accessed February 12, 2014. http://www.quotes.net/quote/5999.

2004. *Napoleon Dynamite.* Directed by Jared Hess. Performed by Efrin Ramirez.

1985. *Pee-wee's Big Adventure.* Directed by Tim Burton. Performed by Paul Ruebens.

Russell, Bertrand. 1957. *Why I Am Not a Christian and Other Essays on Religion and Related Subjects.* New York, N.Y.: Simon & Schuster, Inc.

Saxe, John Godfrey. 2022. *Blind men and the elephant.* May 5. Accessed May 5, 2022. https://www.allaboutphilosophy.org/blind-men-and-the-elephant.htm.

Scofield, C.I. 1984. *The New Scofield Study Bible New International Version.* New York: Oxford University Press.

1998. *Patch Adams.* Directed by Tom Shadyac.

Shuler, Randy. 2010. *Hand me a Dr. Pepper, Please.* Tate Publishing.

Sire, James. 2009. *The Universe Next Door: A Basic Worldview Catalog, Fifth Edition.* Downers Grove, Illinois: InterVarsity Press.

Solzhenitsyn, Alexsandr. 1974. *The Gulag Archipelago 1918–1956.* New York City: Harper and Row.

Strobel, Lee. 2004. *The Case for a Creator.* Grand Rapids, MI: Zondervan.

Sweet, Leonard. 2001. *Carpe Manana: Is your church ready to seize tommorrow?* Grand Rapids, Michigan: Zondervan.

Taylor, Steve. 1984. *Guilty by Association from Meltdown.* Comp. Steve Taylor.

Taylor, Steve. 1987. *I Predict 1990.* Comp. Steve Taylor.

U2. 1987. *Bullet the Blue Sky from The Joshua Tree.* Cond. Bono. Comp. Bono.

USA Today. 2007. *25 Most Memorable Quotes.* April 2. Accessed June 8, 2012. http://usatoday30.usatoday.com/news/top25-quotes.htm.

Viereck, G. S. 1929. "What Life Means to Einstein." *Saturday Evening Post,* October 26: 60.

1998. *What Dreams May Come.* Directed by Vincent Ward.

1989. *Dead Poets Society.* Directed by Peter Weir.

Wright, N.T. 2006. *Simply Christian: Why Christianity Makes Sense.* New York City, N.Y.: Harper Collins Publishers.

Youtube. 1998. "What is the evidence for/against God?" *Youtube.com.* April 3. http://www.youtube.com/watch?v=9qT1pp_jCUw.

Zhao, Christina. 2019. "NBC's Chuck Todd Faces Backlash for Highlighting Letter Comparing Bible Story to Trump Falsehoods and 'Fairy Tales.'" *Newsweek.* December 29. Accessed December 30, 2019. https://www.newsweek.com/nbcs-chuck-todd-faces-backlash-highlighting-letter-comparing-bible-story-trump-falsehoods-1479569.

Darrin Crow is the founding pastor of HEART of Junction, a church in Grand Junction Colorado. He holds degrees from Colorado Christian University and Regis University. In addition to pastoring, Darrin served as an adjunct professor for Colorado Christian University for nearly two decades. Darrin has also worked as a missionary to the campus of Colorado Mesa University since 1985 as the director of a ministry called Christian Challenge. His ministerial résumé includes over thirty trips overseas and extensive personal and group counseling opportunities. He also serves on the board of directors of She Has A Name (shehasaname.info), a non-profit organization that helps to work against poverty-based prostitution in Nairobi by significantly helping girls one at a time from point of contact through college graduation. He is married to Stephanie and has two adult children, Liesen and Blythe.

Understanding Theism 101 is the first entry of at least four books in what will be a series of entry-level looks at various aspects of Christian life. Look for the next book, *Understanding Biblical Mental Health 101* by early 2023. *Understanding Church 101* and *Understanding the Bible 101* will follow.

THE END

CPSIA information can be obtained
at www.ICGtesting.com
Printed in the USA
LVHW110825120922
728125LV00001B/5